TREASURES

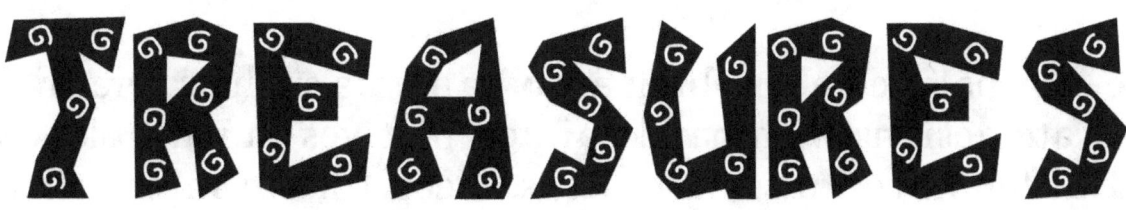

THE PRE-COLUMBIAN ART COLOURING BOOK

Illustrated by Jorge Lulić

Published by Jorge Lulić Fine Art and Print Publications Alicante, Spain.
The book author retains sole copyright to the design and artwork in this book.
www.jorgelulic.com

Colouring tips:

- When it comes to colouring, think about using all of the space you have to fill with whichever colours you like the most. For the leafs, stems and branches try differents shades of green, yellows, blues and browns to give your picture more depth.

- The original pre-coloumbian art ornaments such as ceramics had intricate designs with hand painted motives in red, gold, orange and different contrasting tones, so keep this in mind when you choose your colours.

- Use either pencils or markers and always test your markers or pencils before your start colouring.

- Remember the ink from markers might bleed through the page, or the inks might run, so slip another piece of paper behind the page you're colouring to protect the page behind.

- Pencils will allow you to blend colours and are very good for fine details. If you like using pencils, buy the biggest selection of colours you can, and keep them well sharpened.

- Lastly: Study the picture carefully before you start, relax, take your time, and enjoy the process of colouring, and watch the pre-columbian art designs come to life!

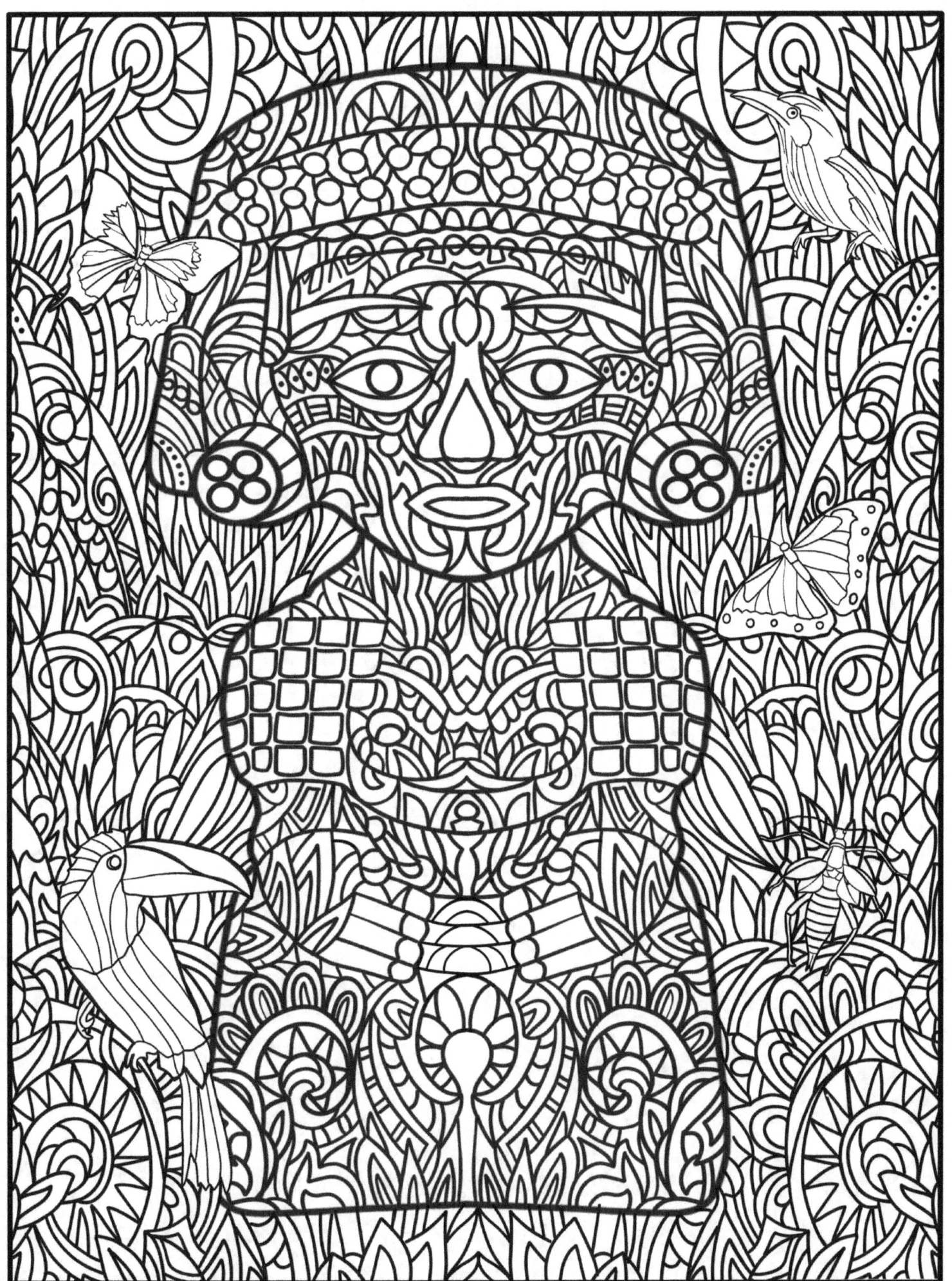

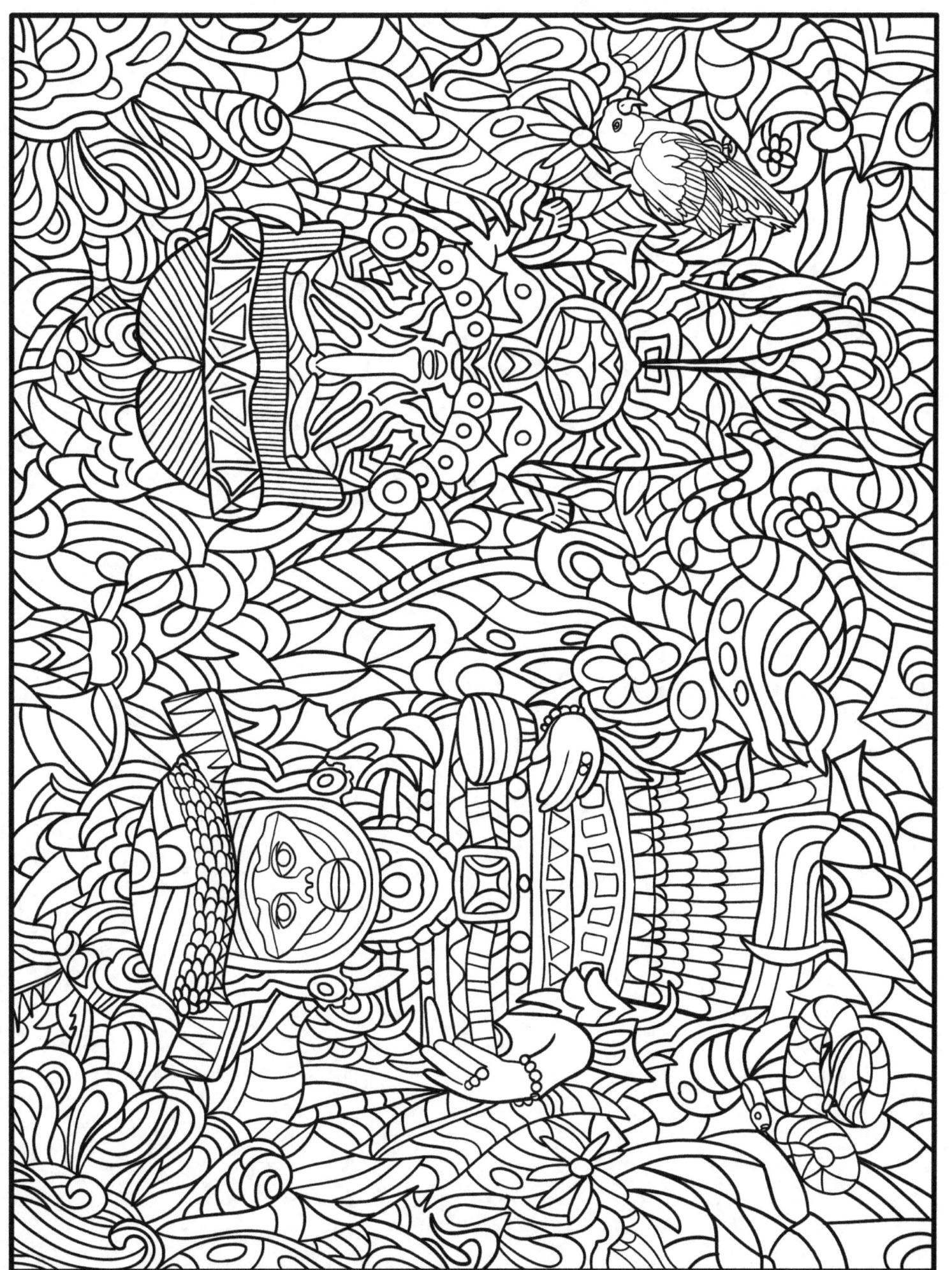

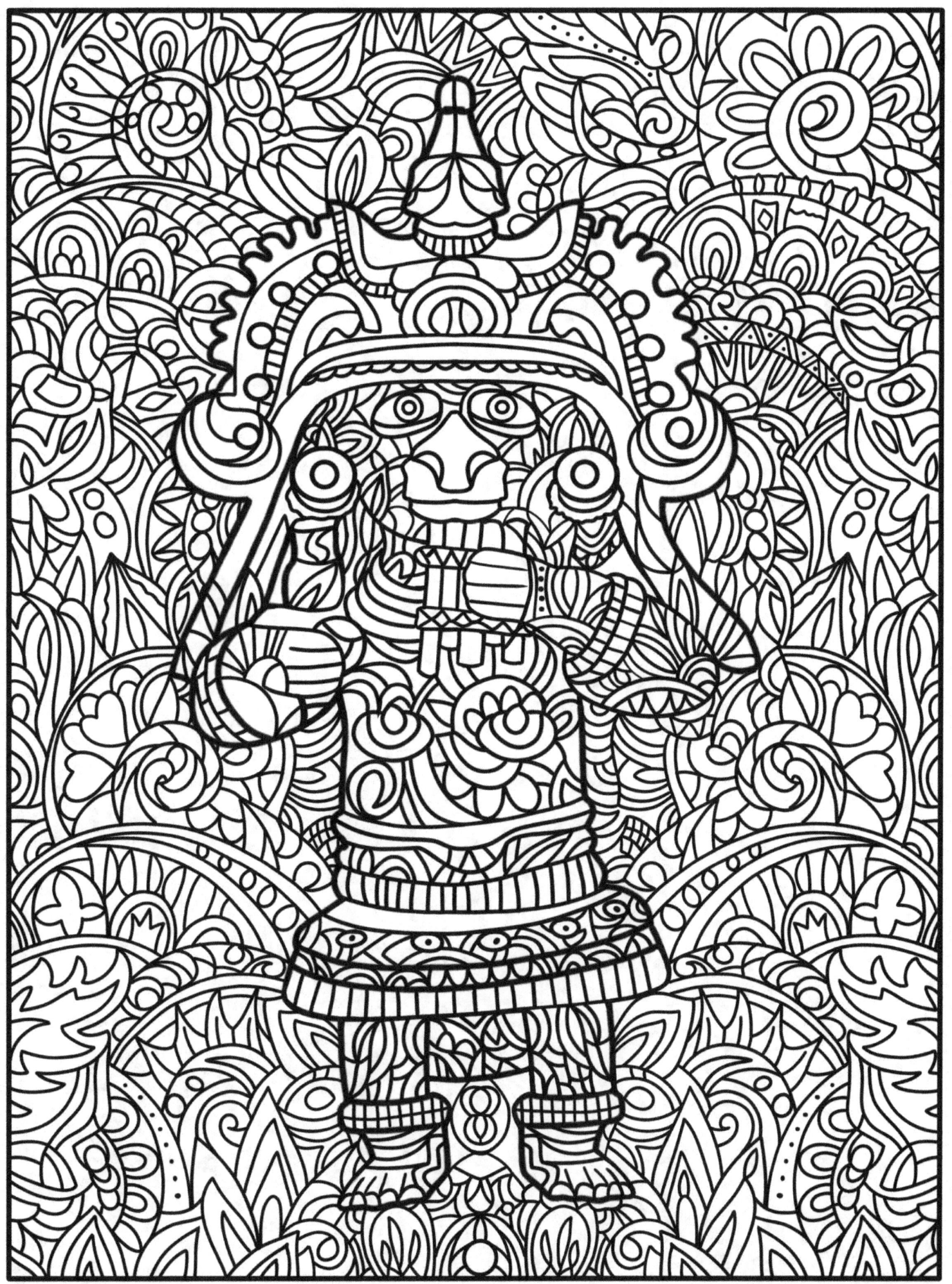

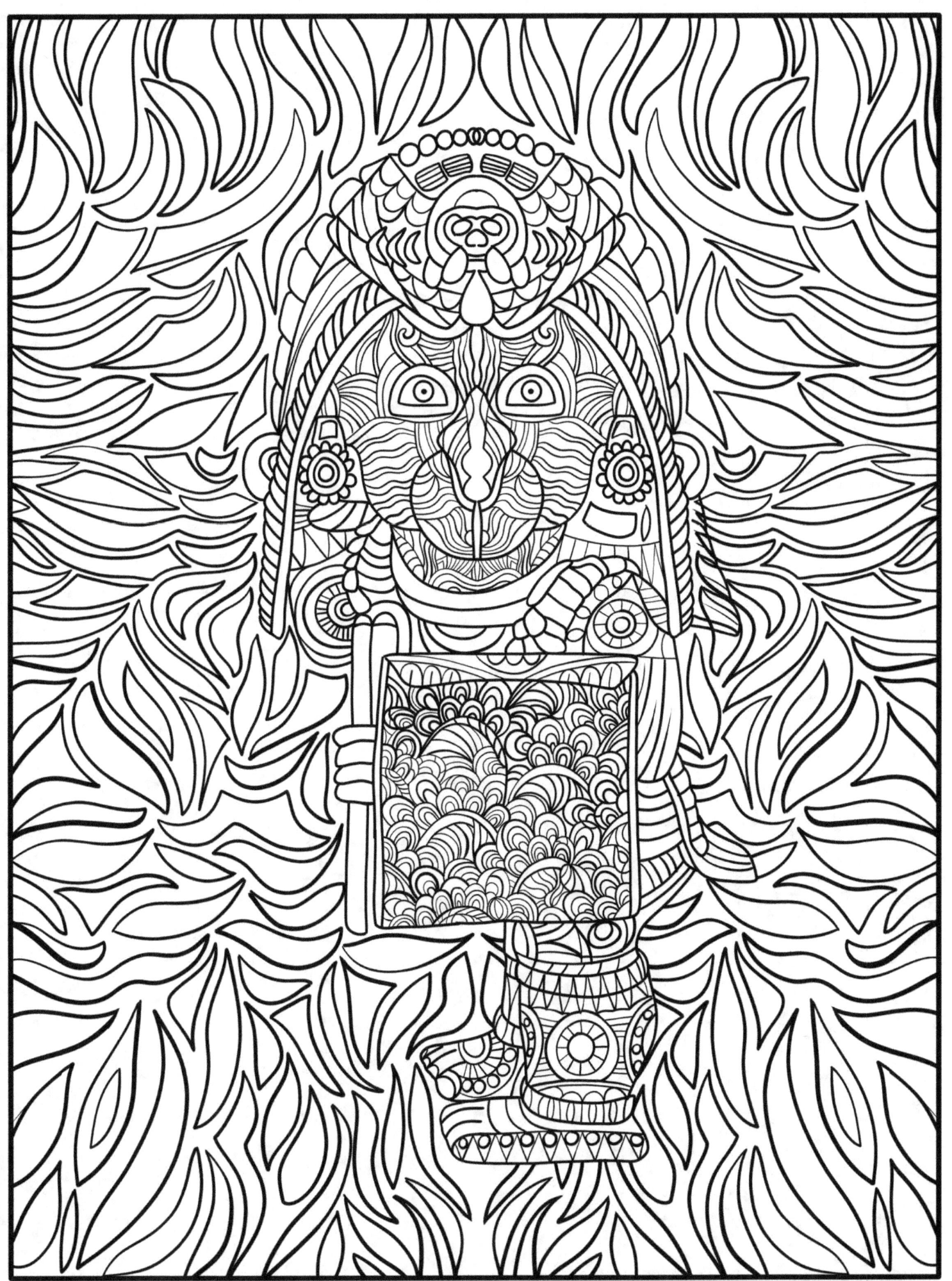

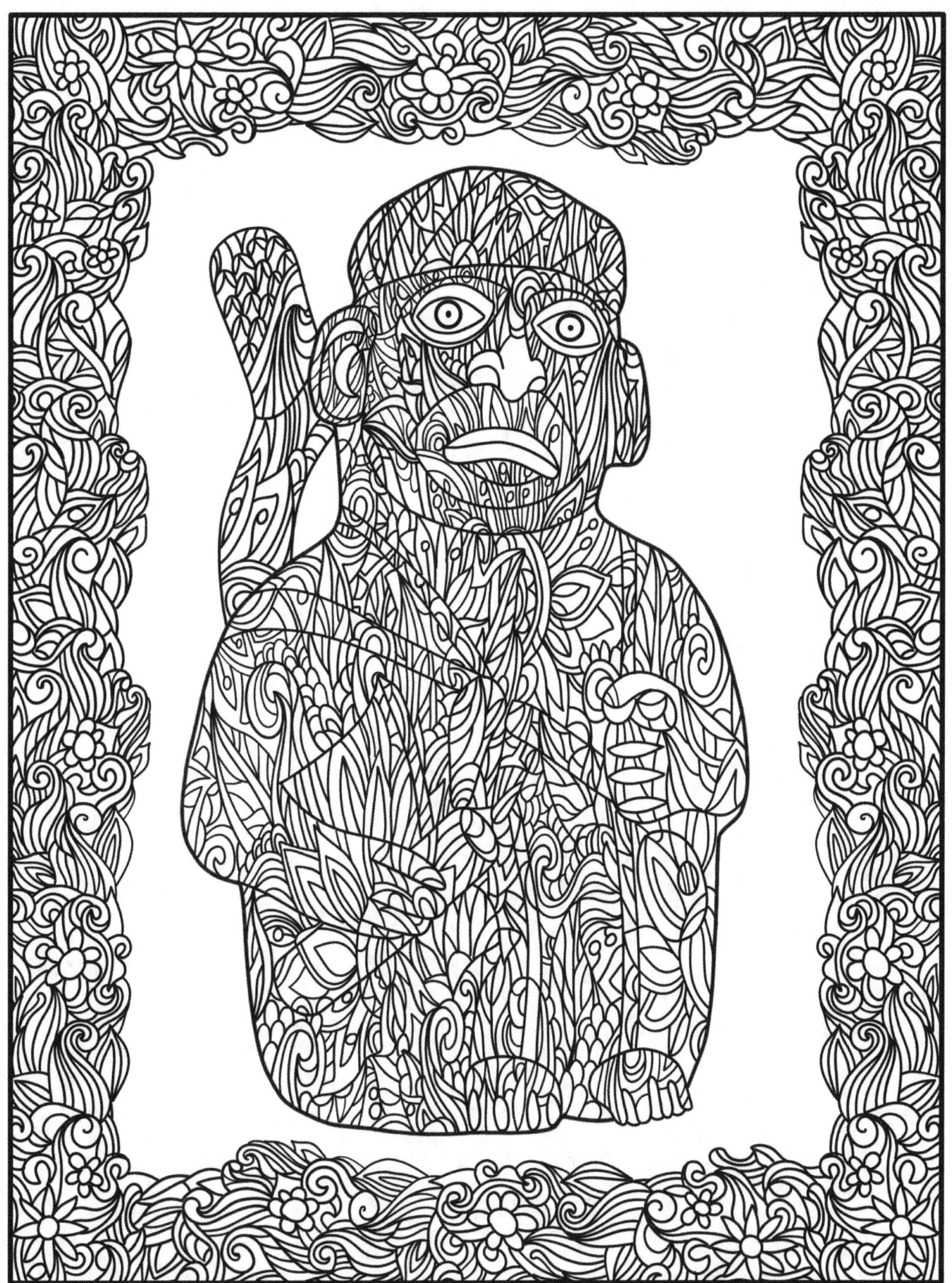

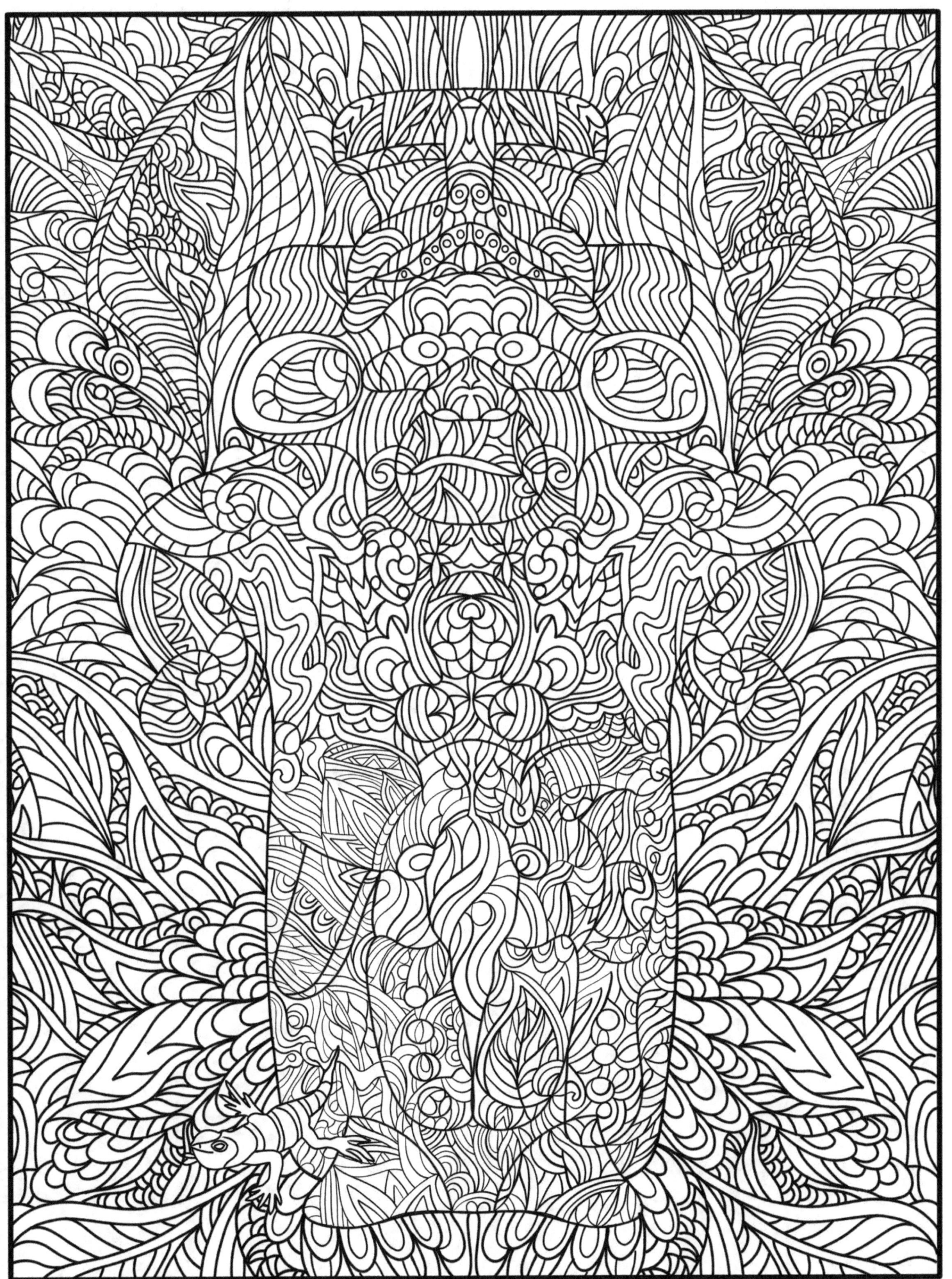

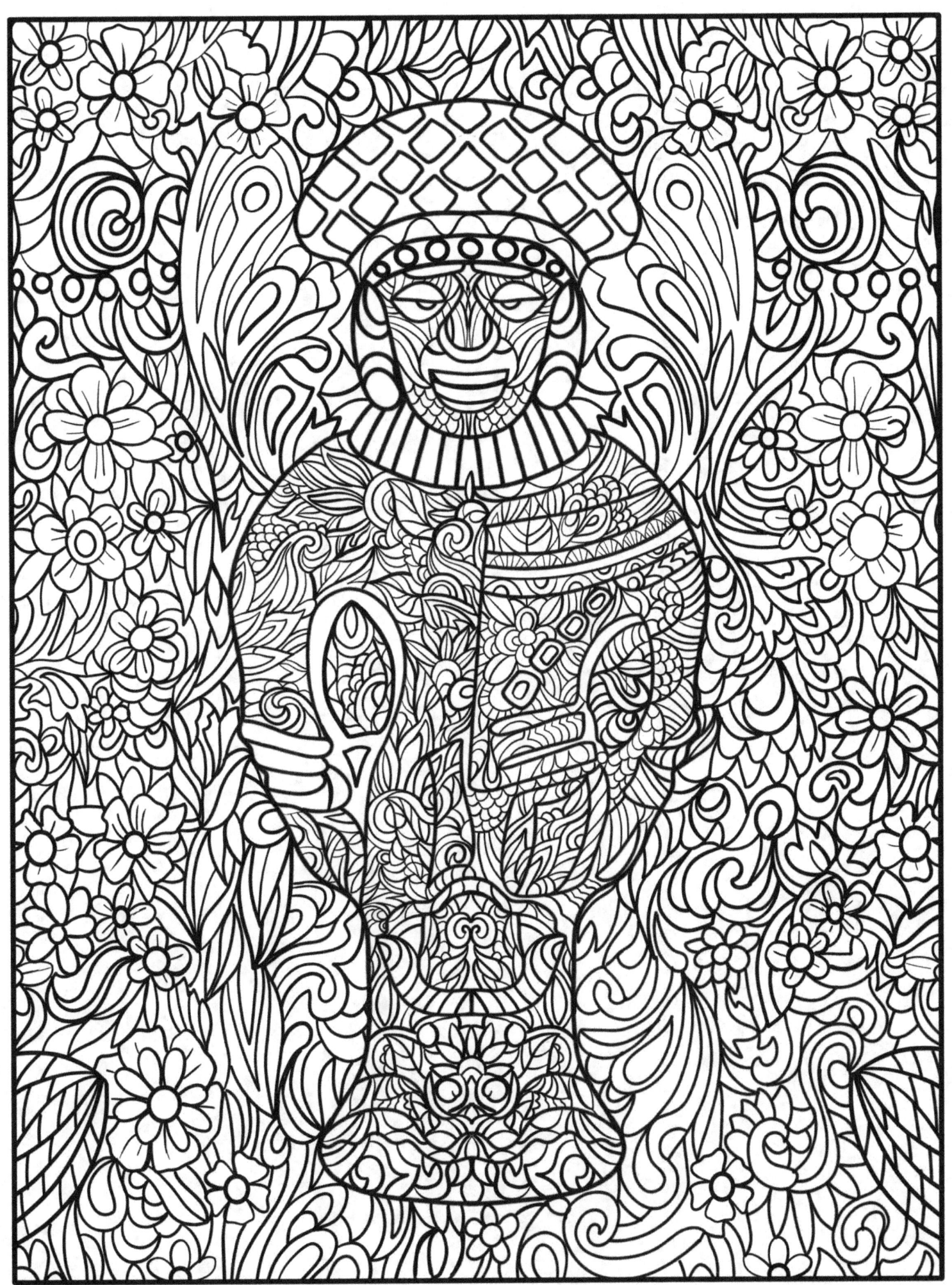

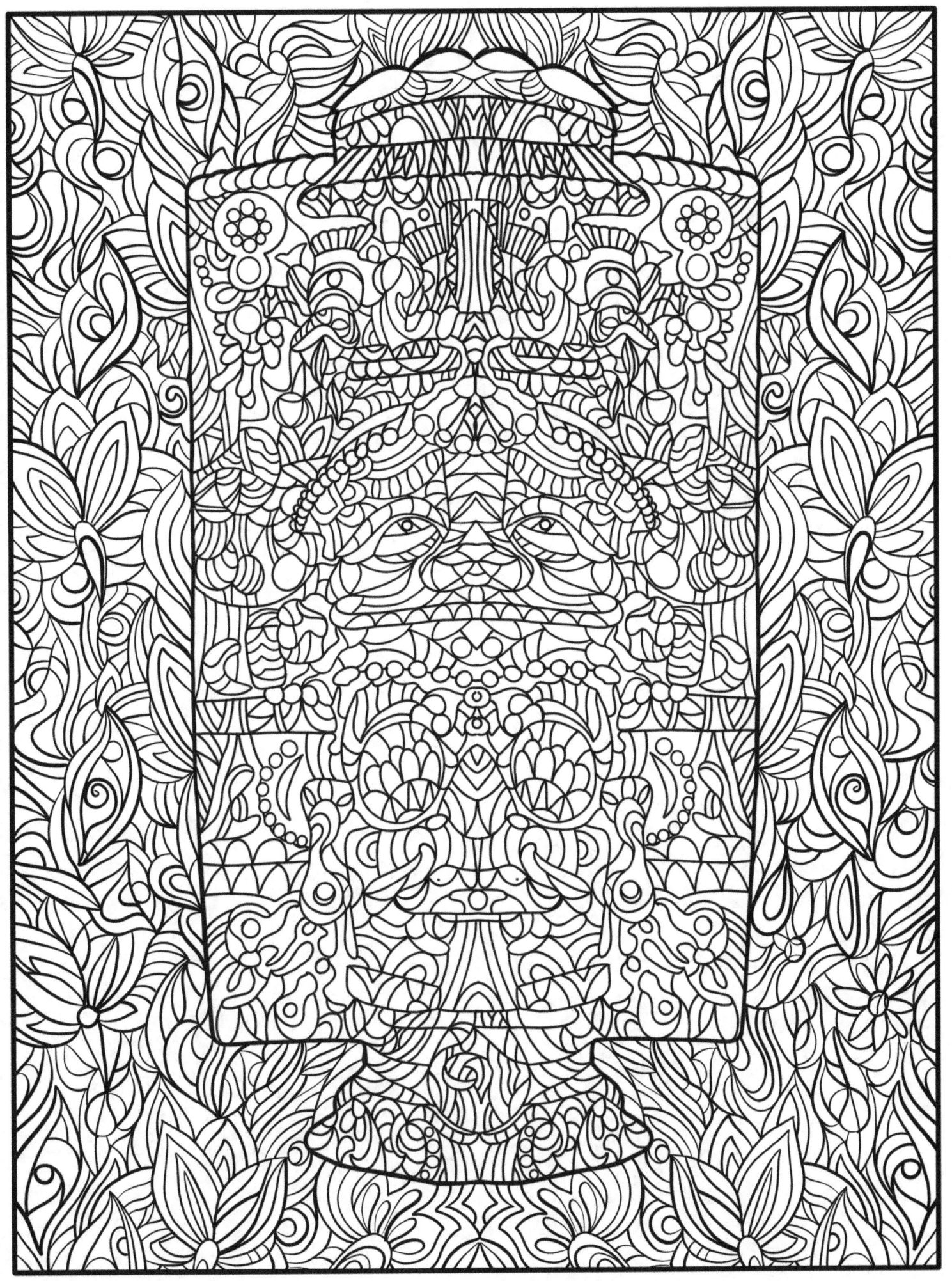

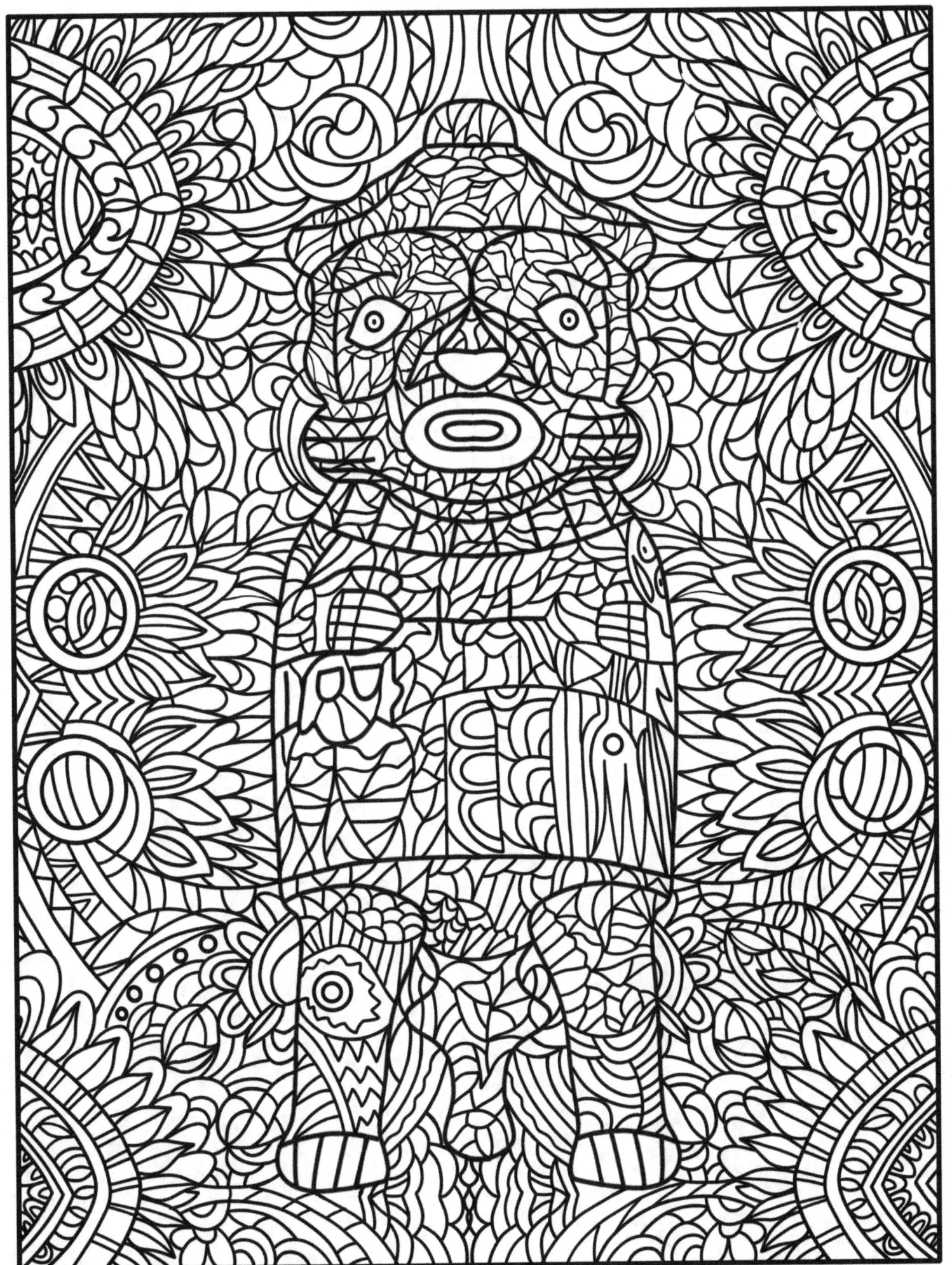

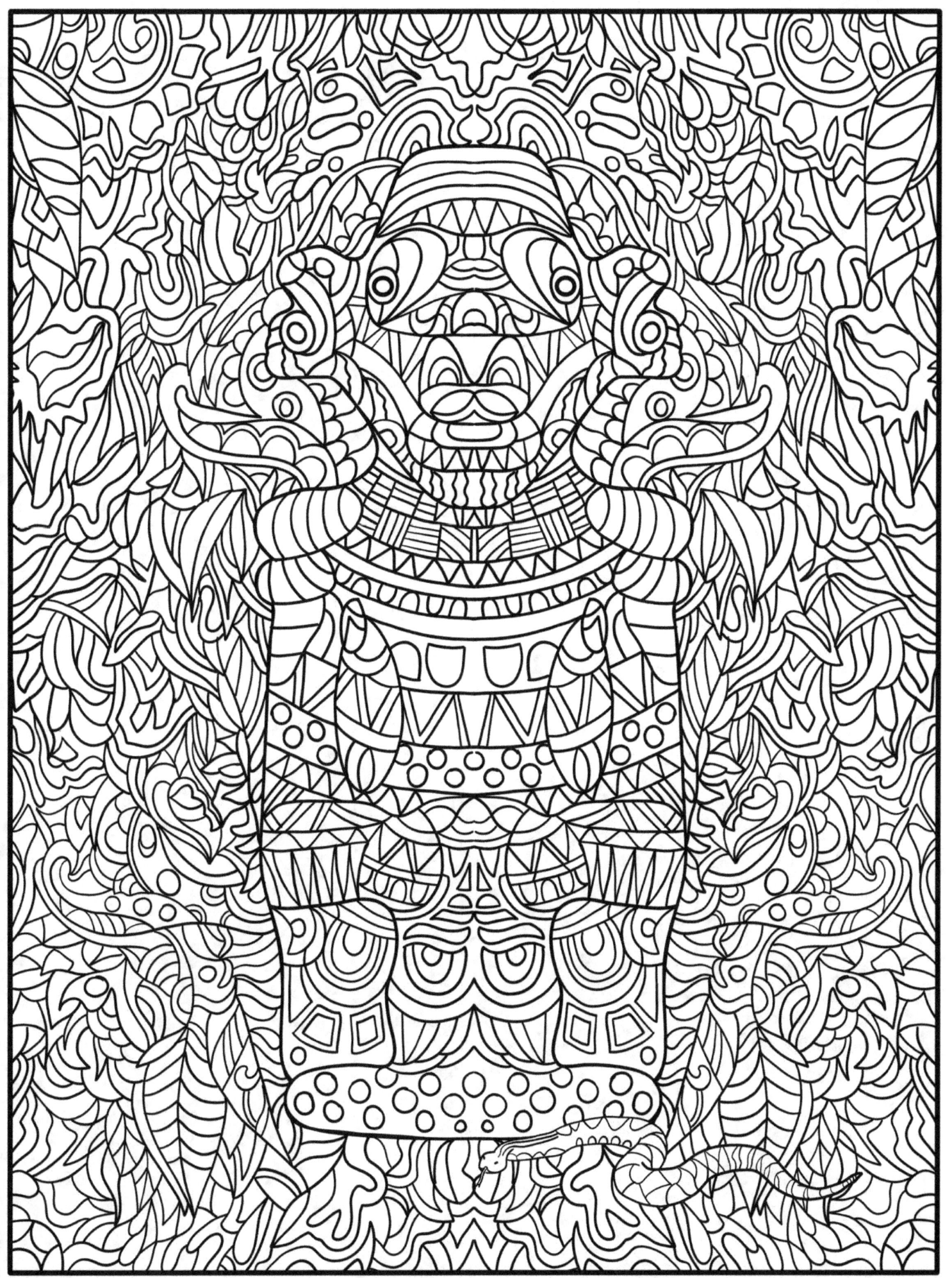

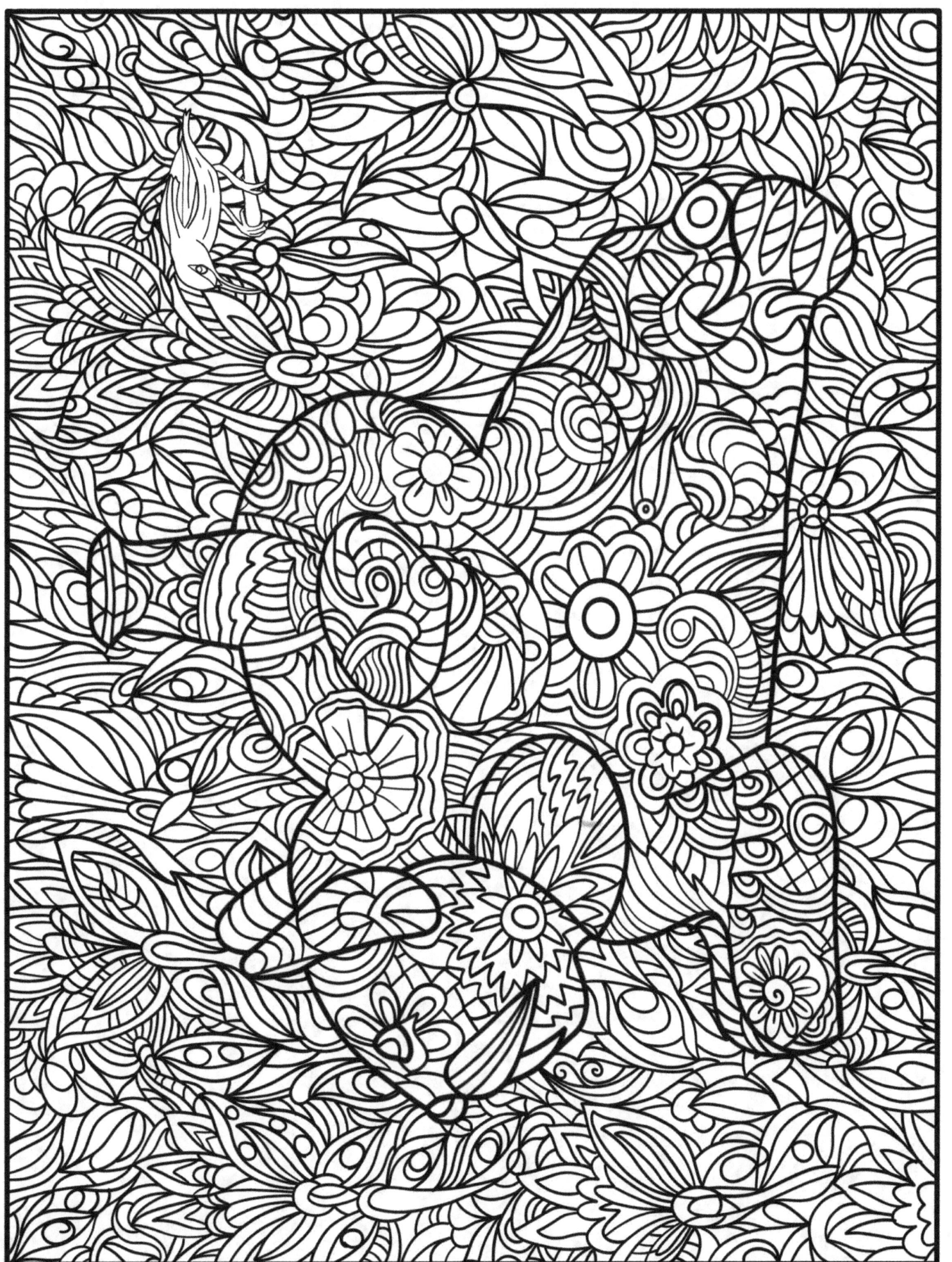

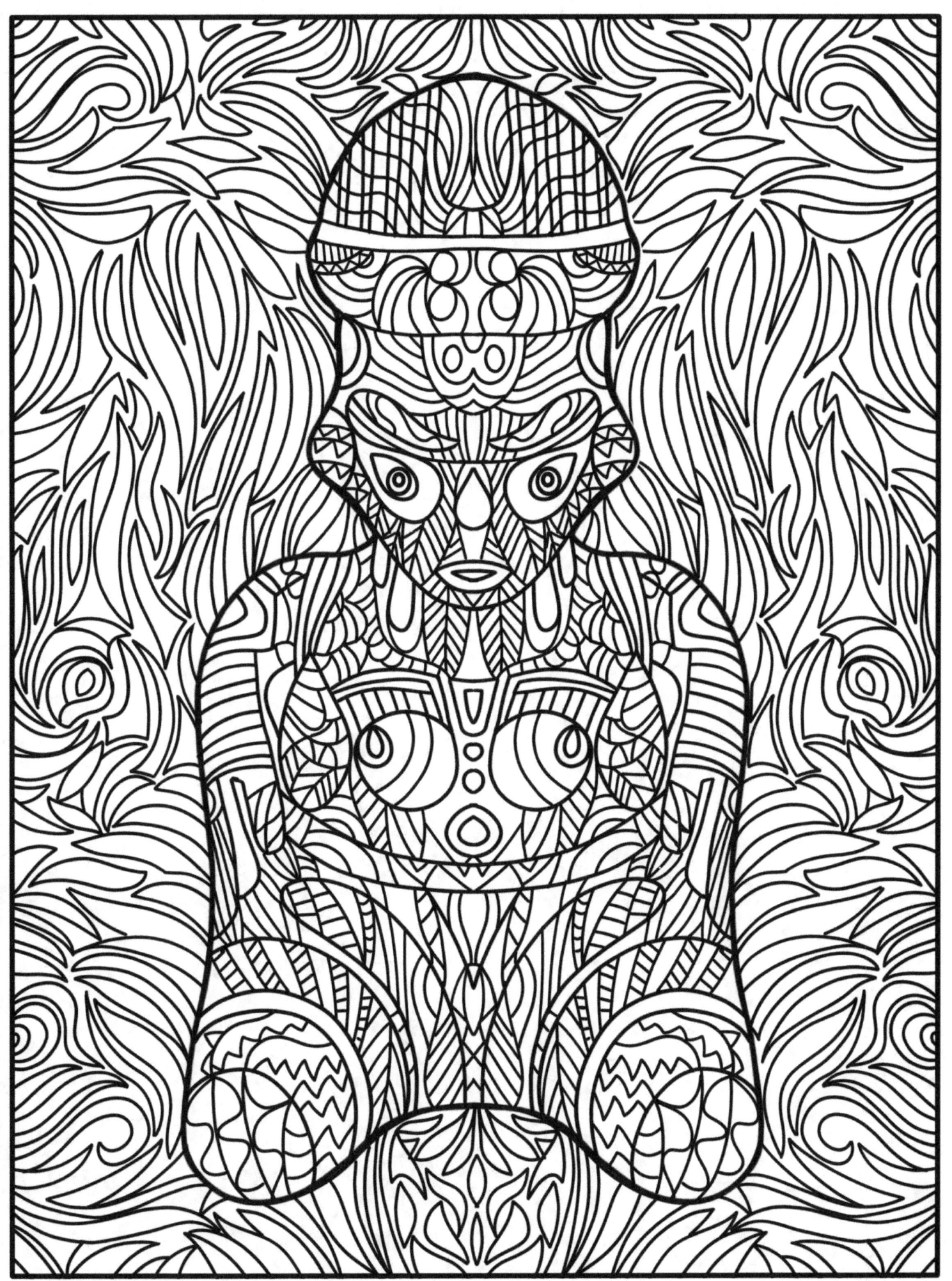

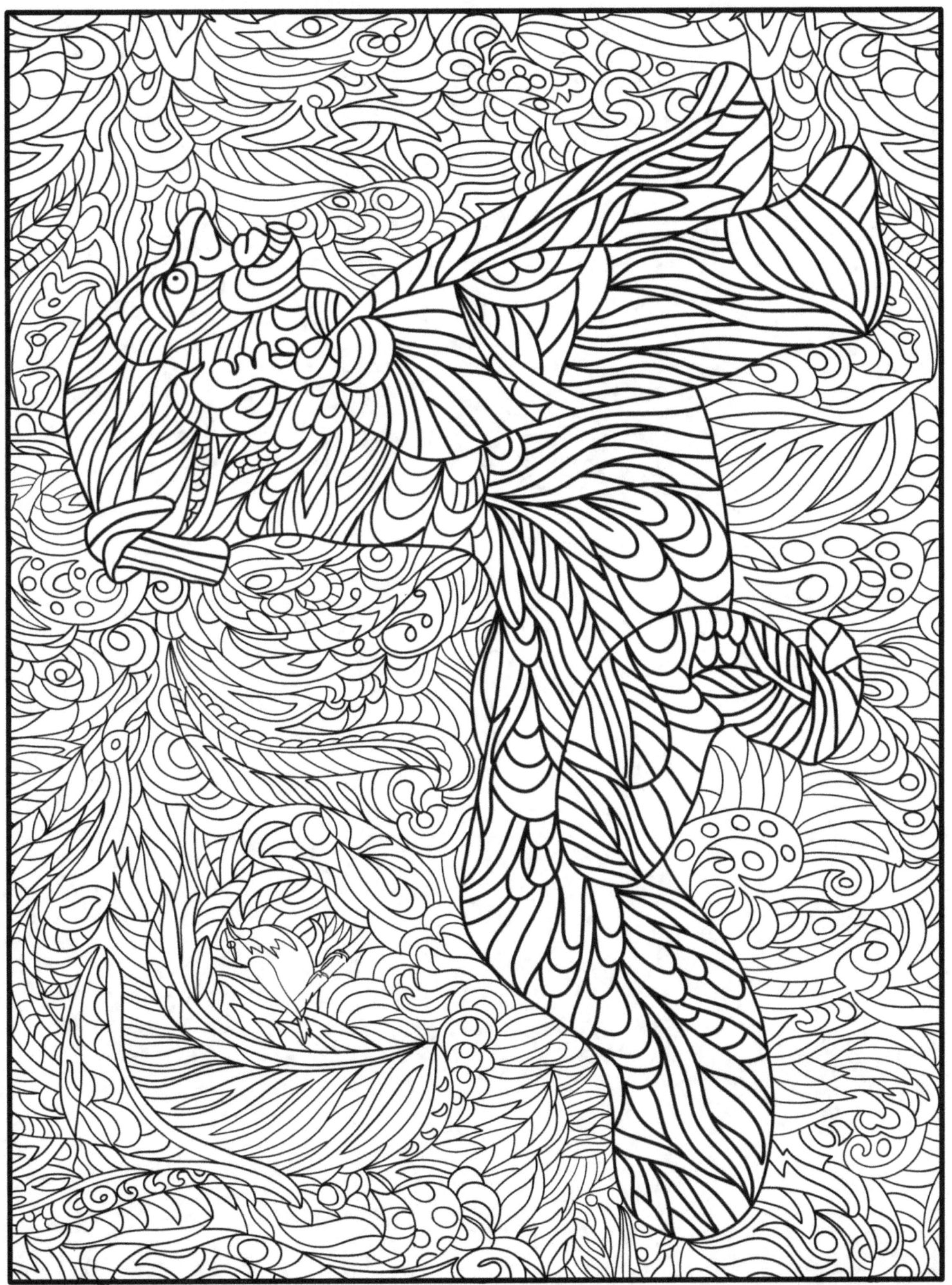

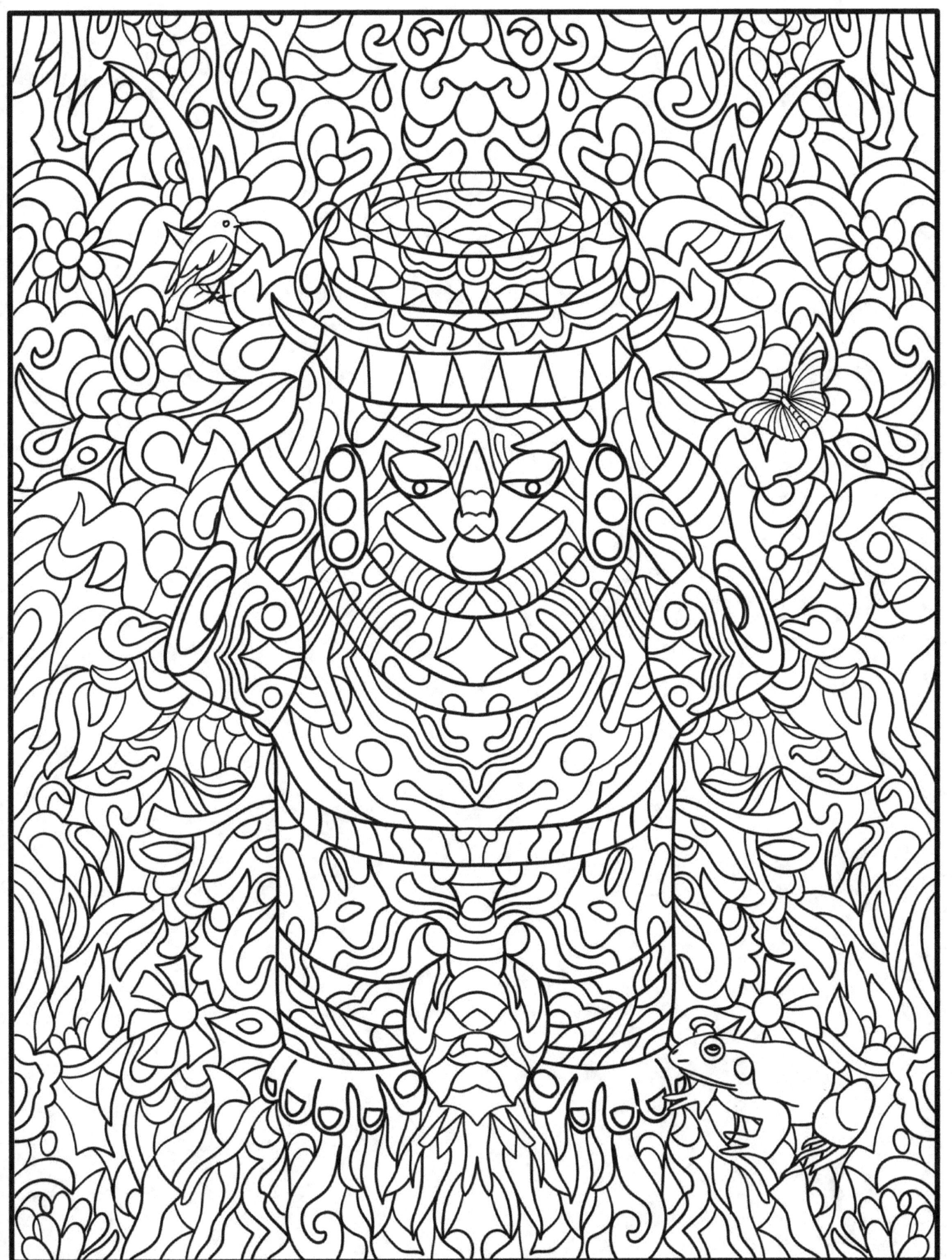

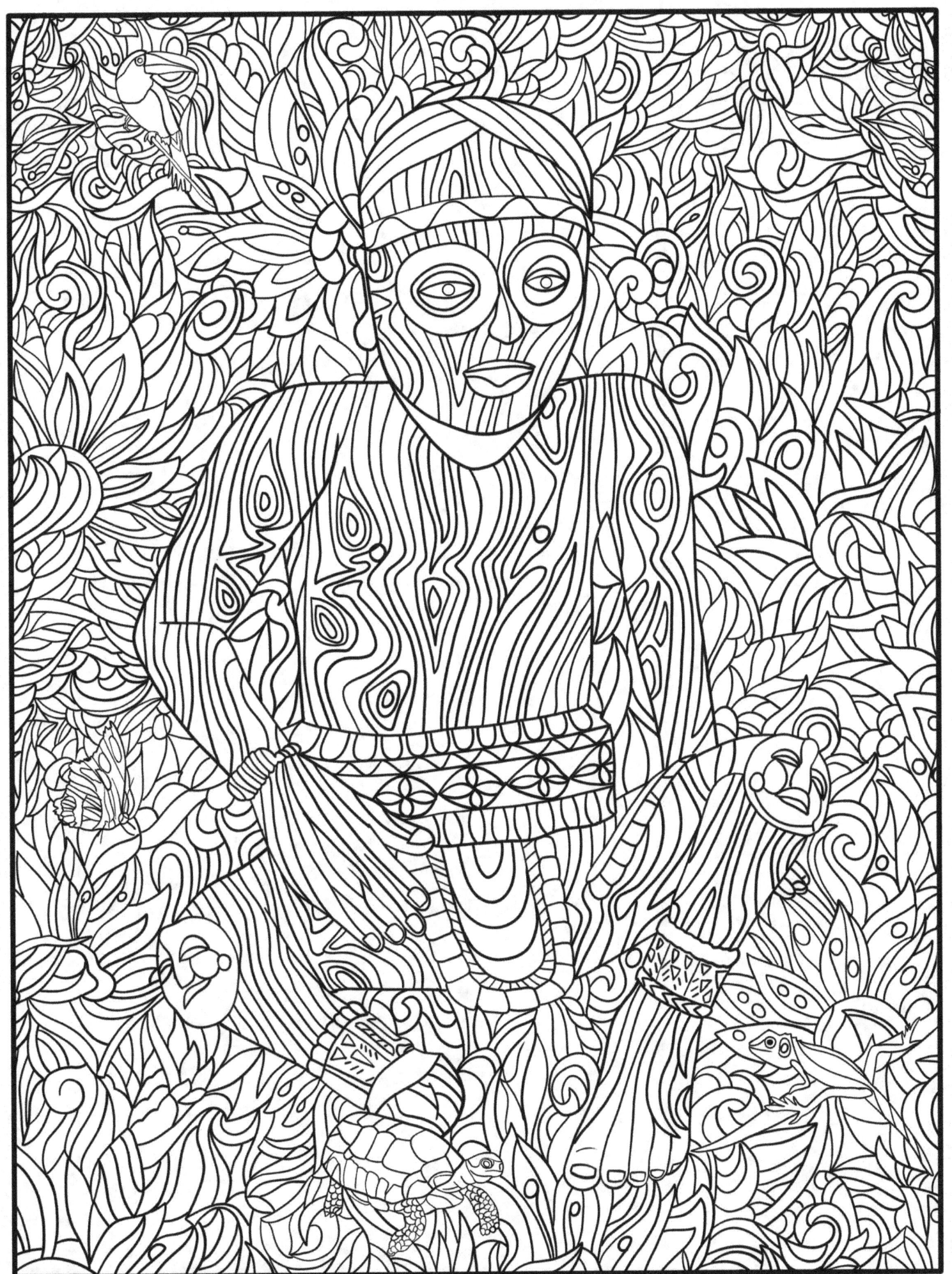

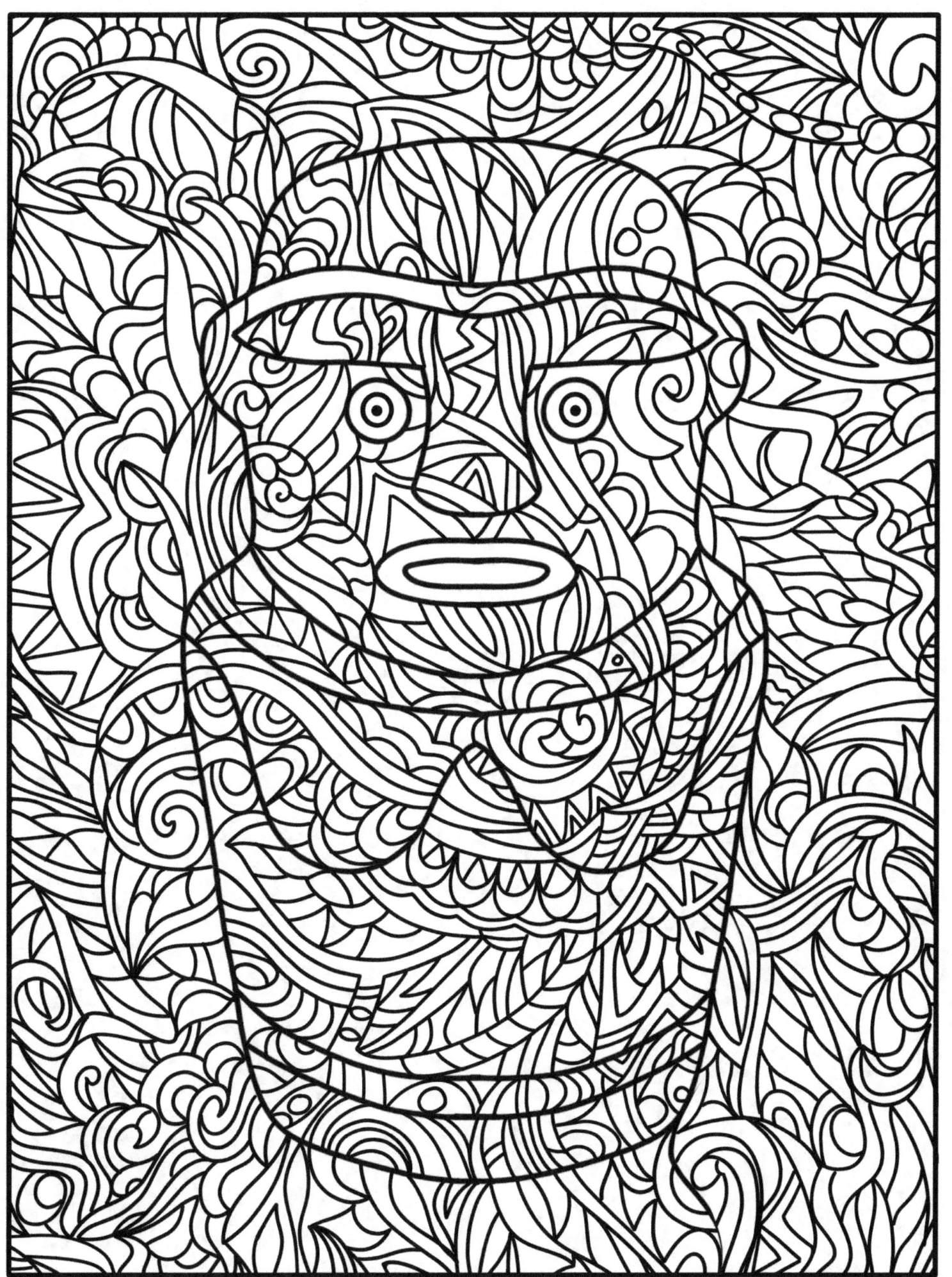

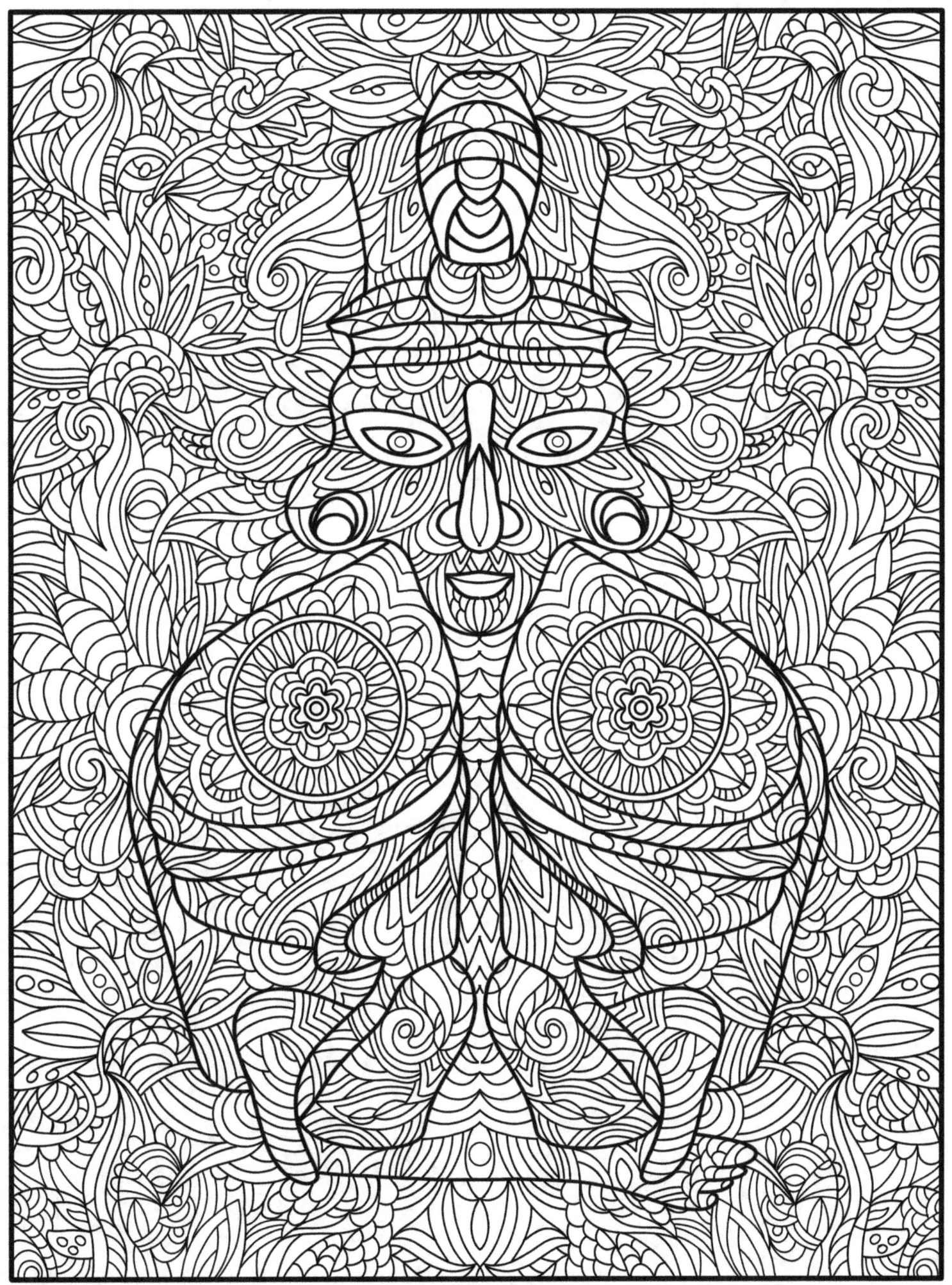

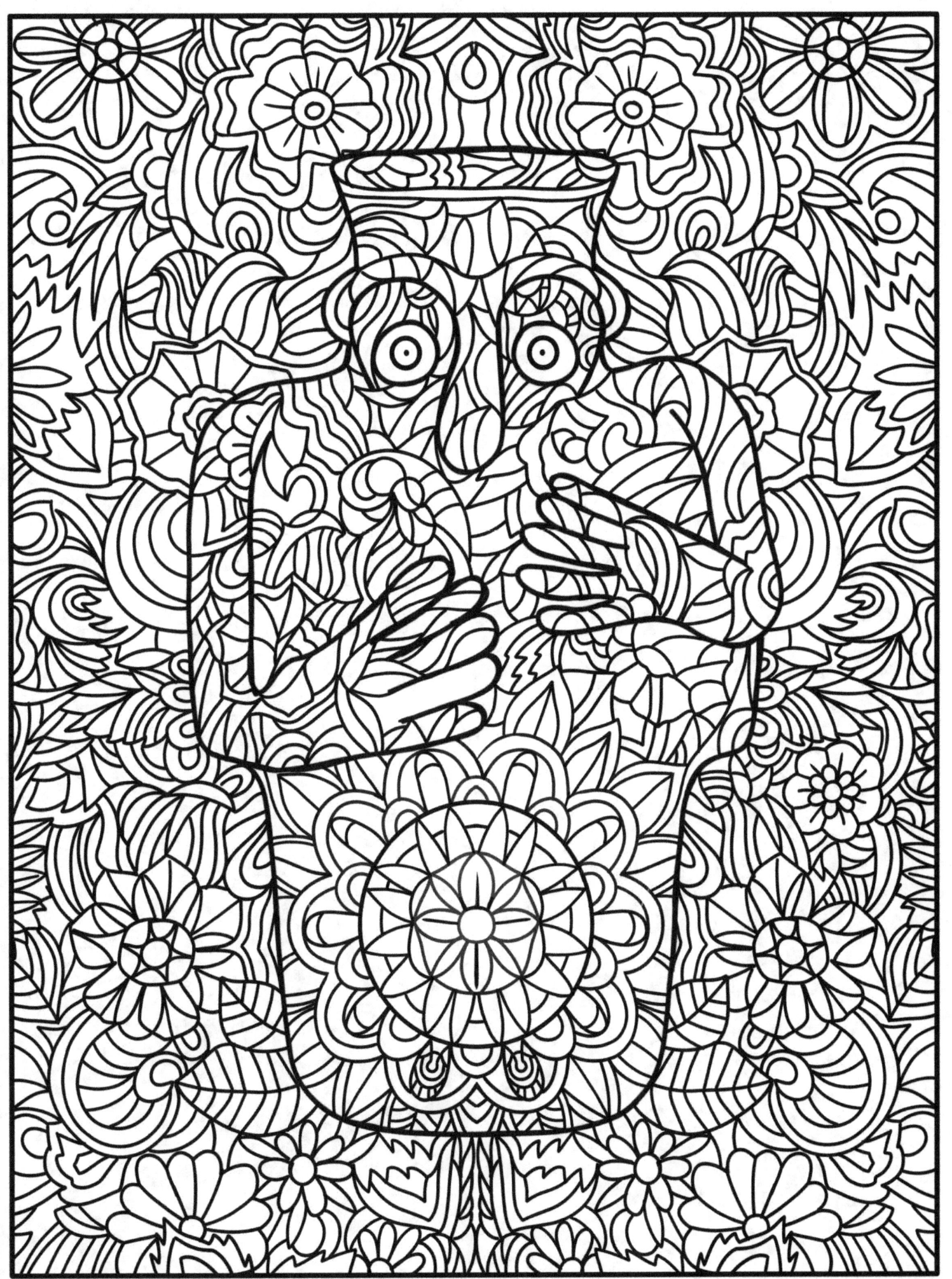

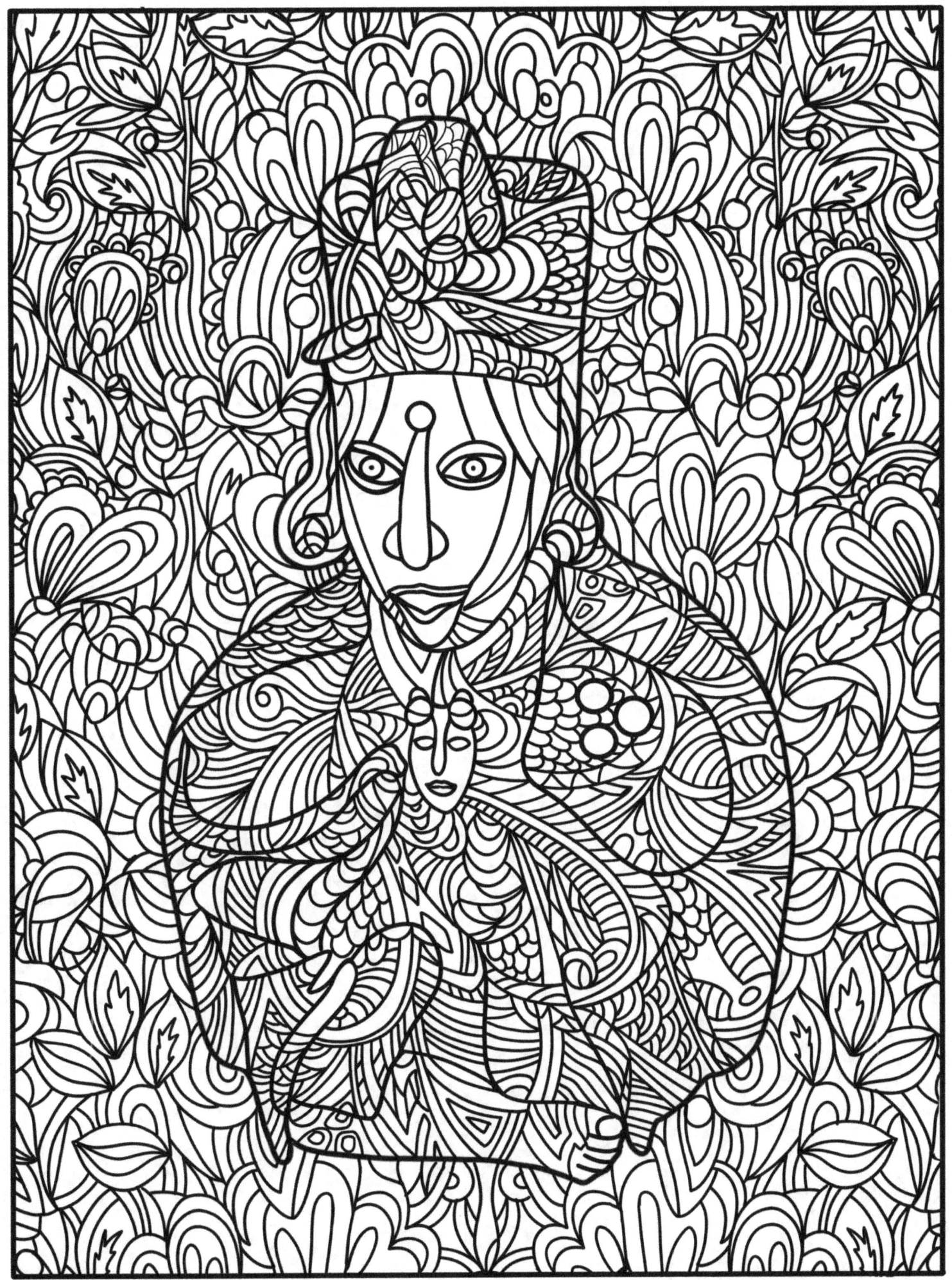

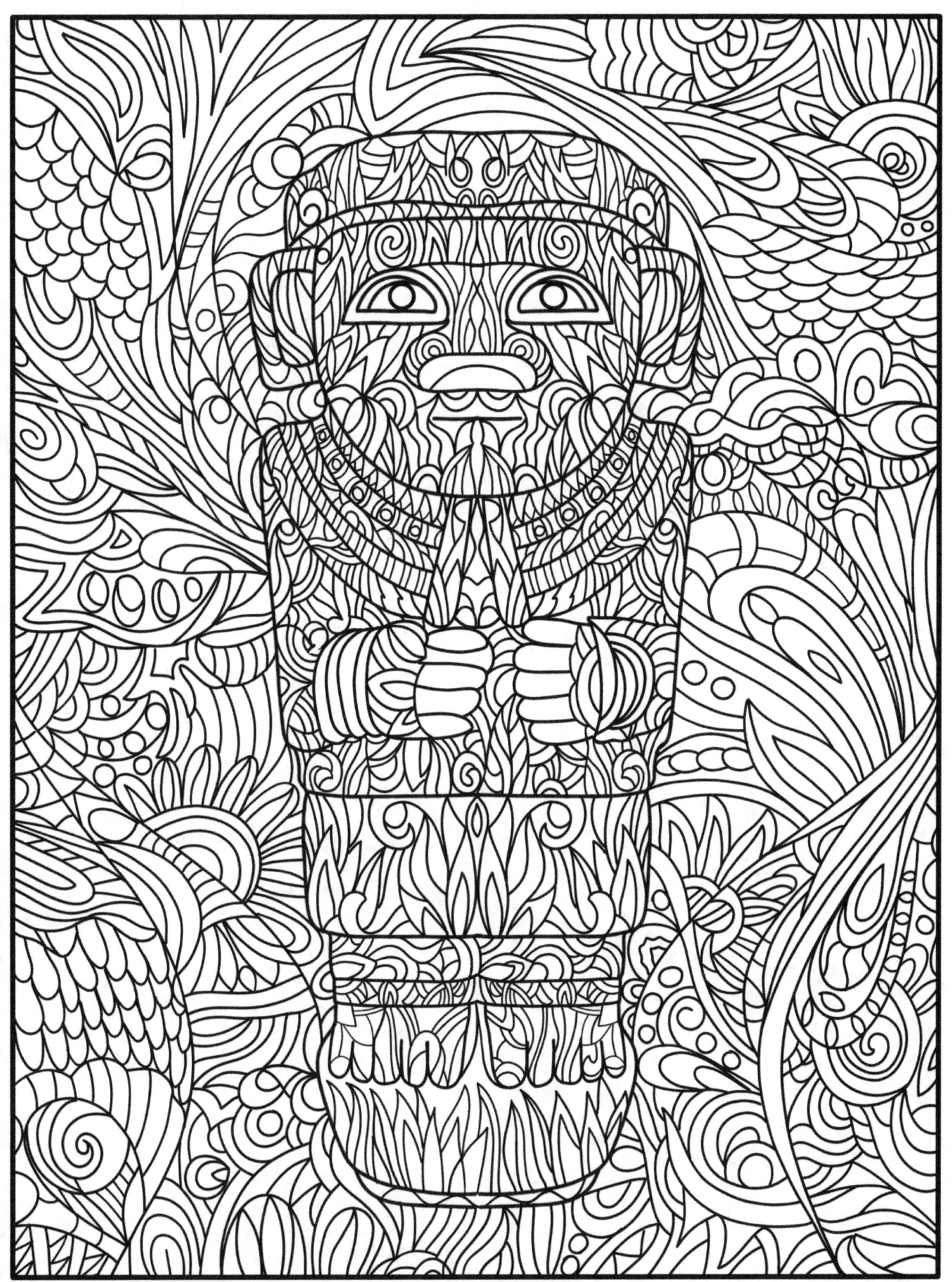

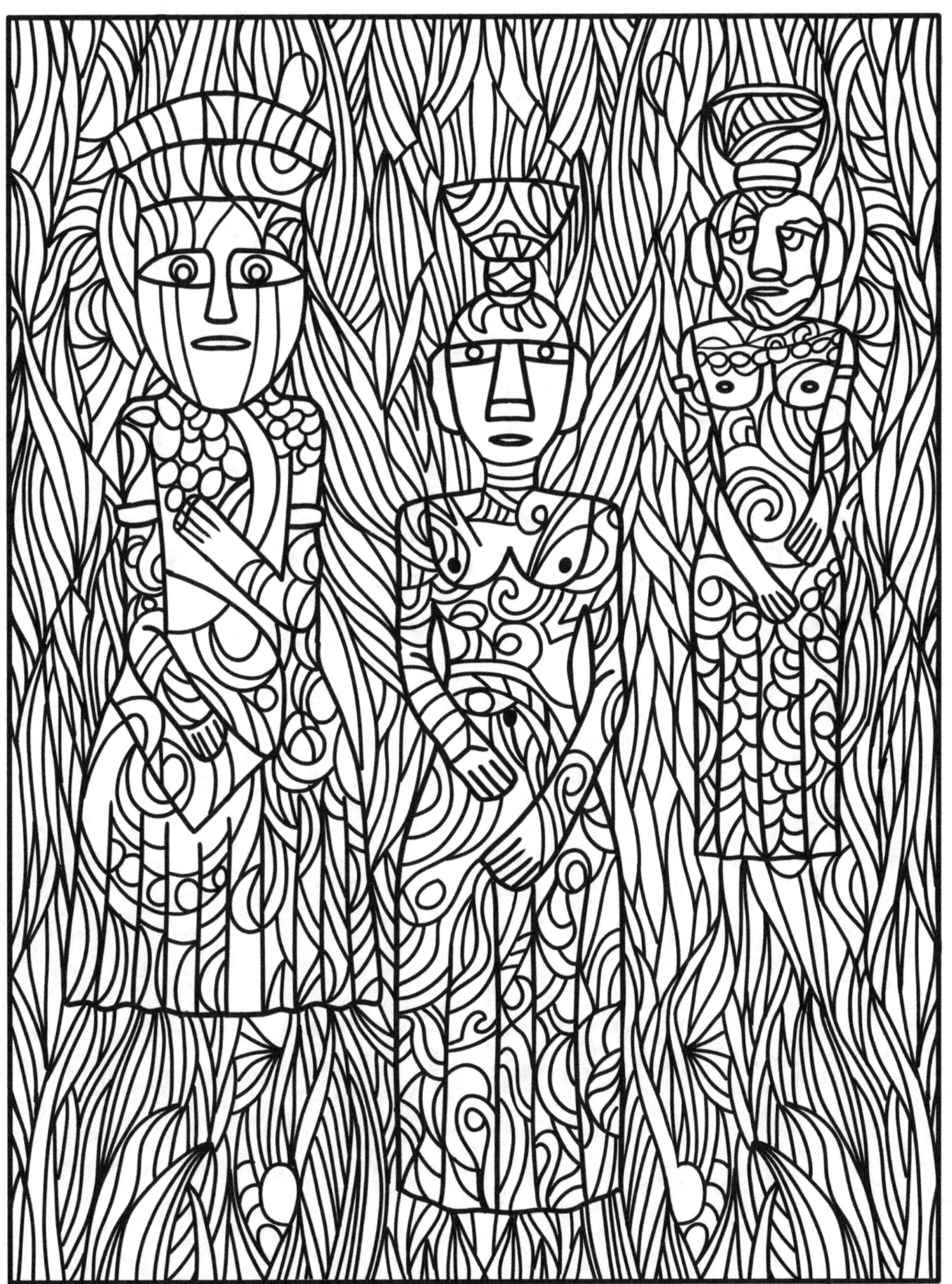

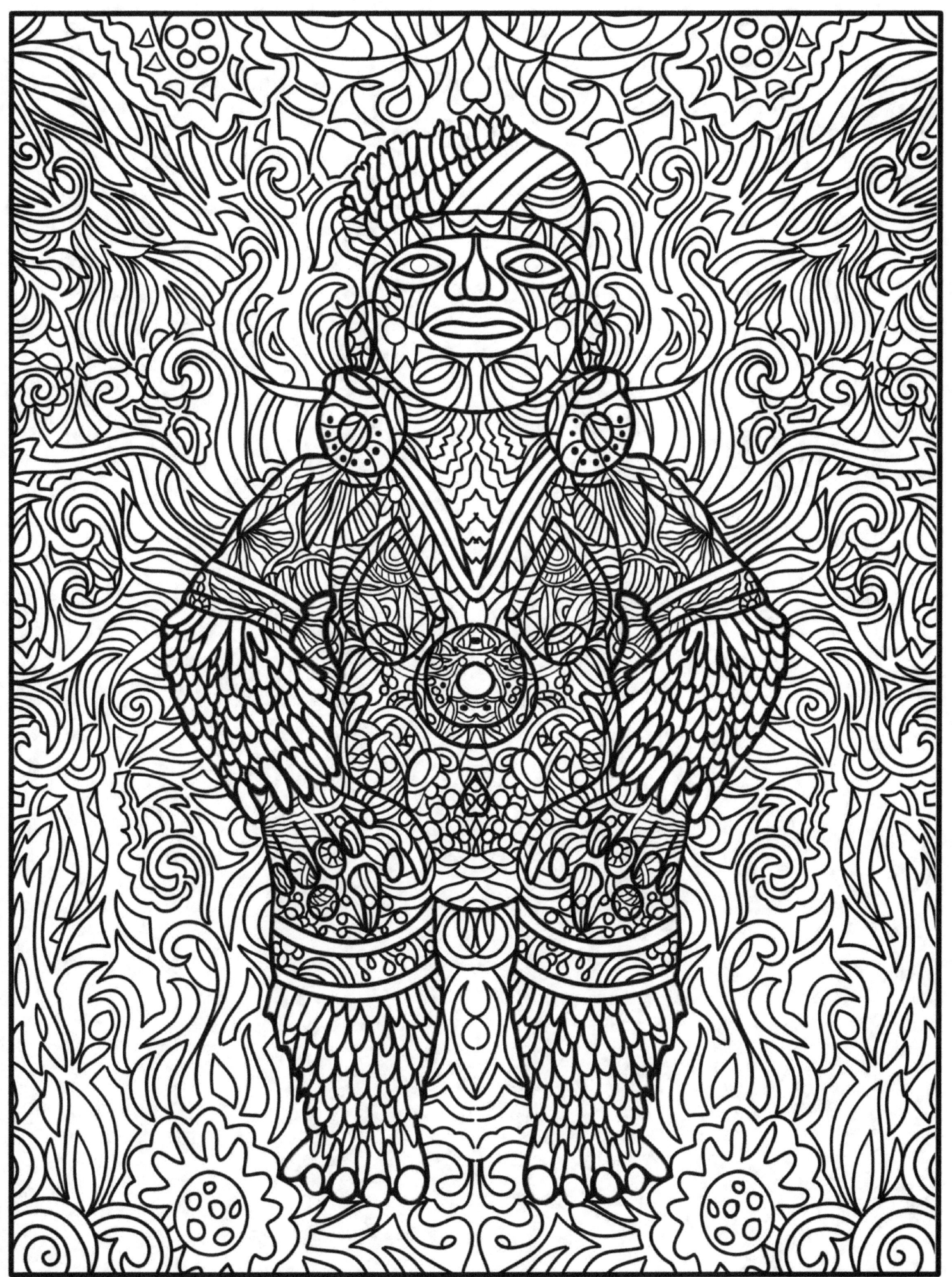

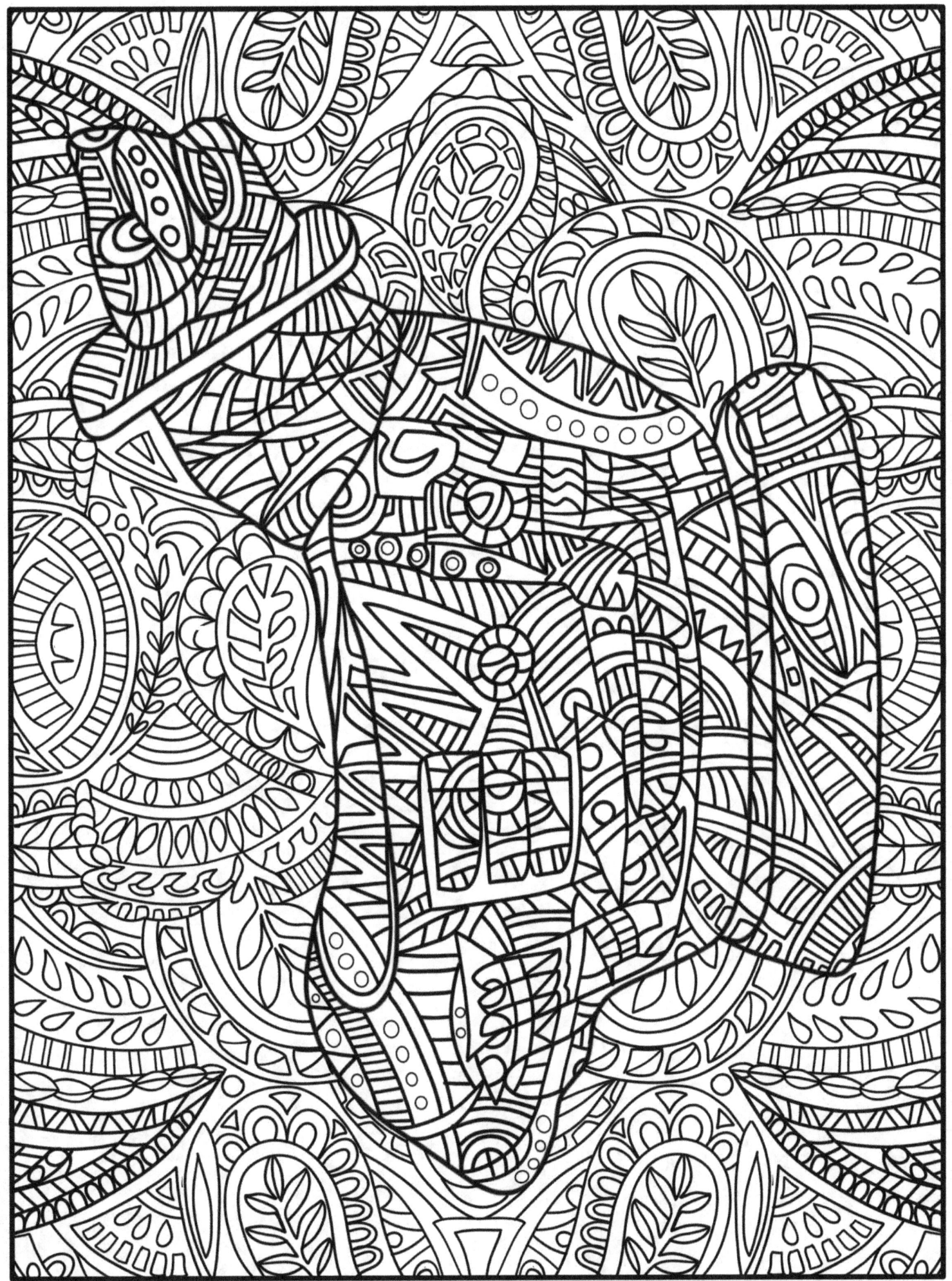

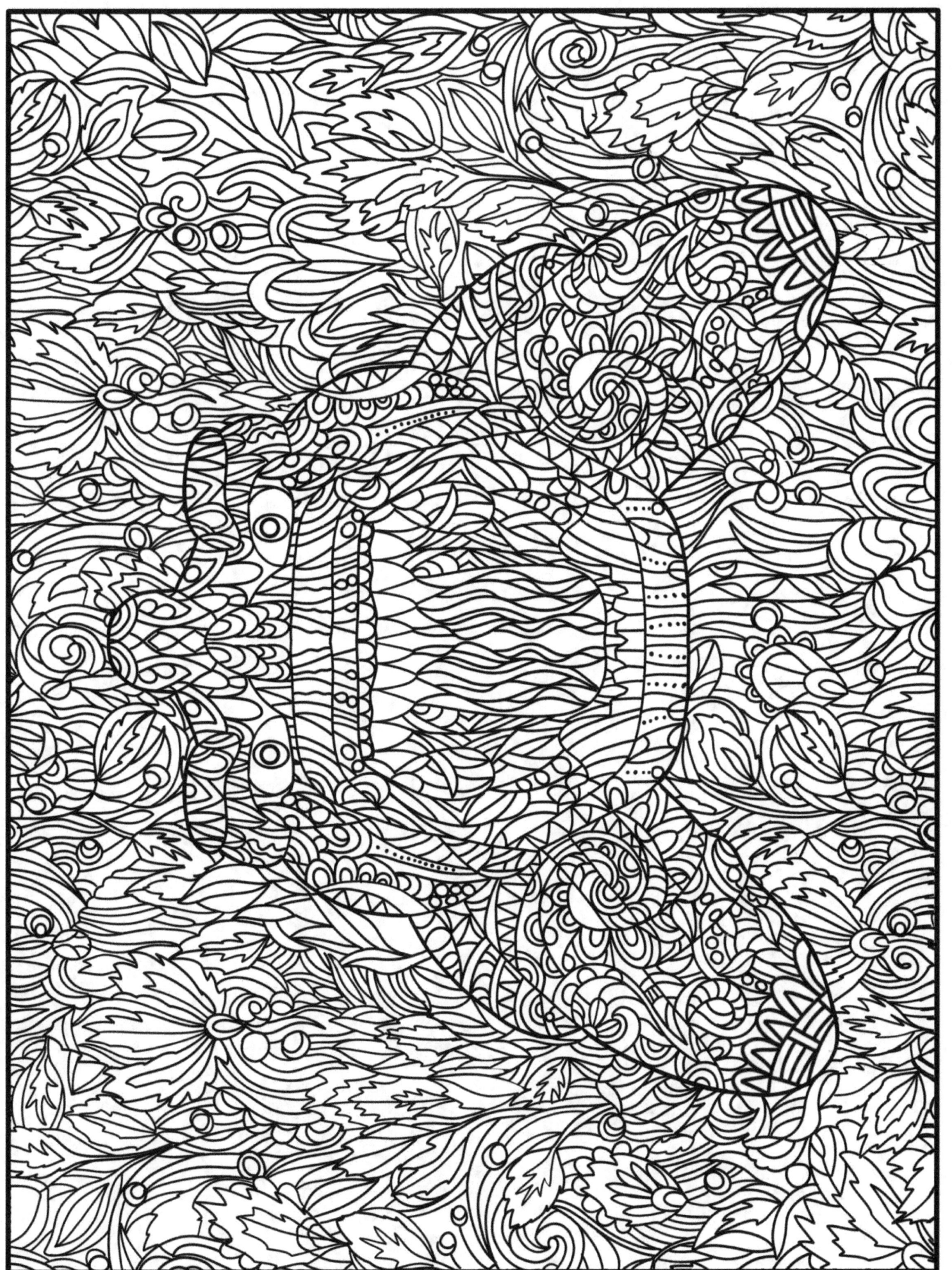

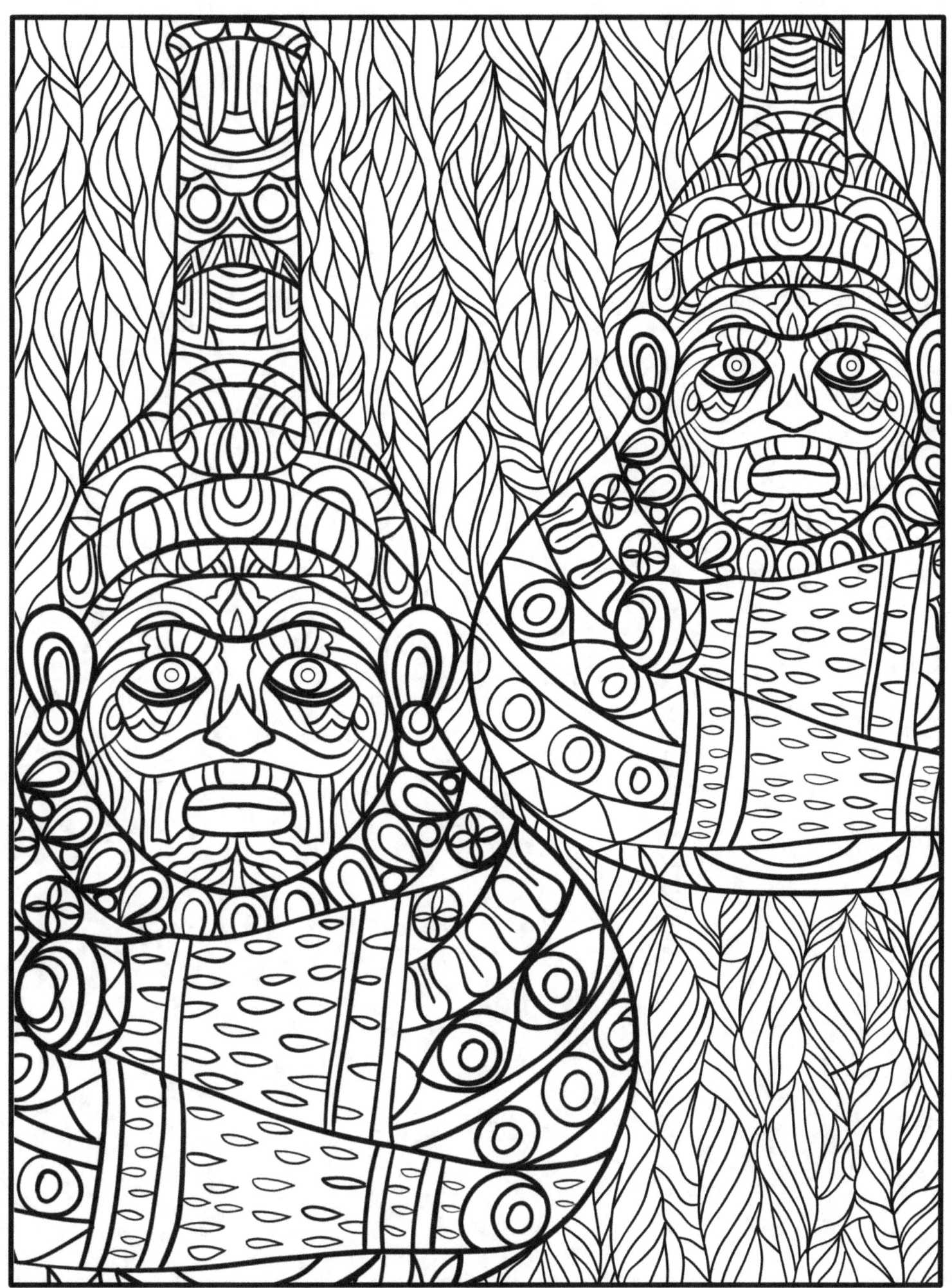

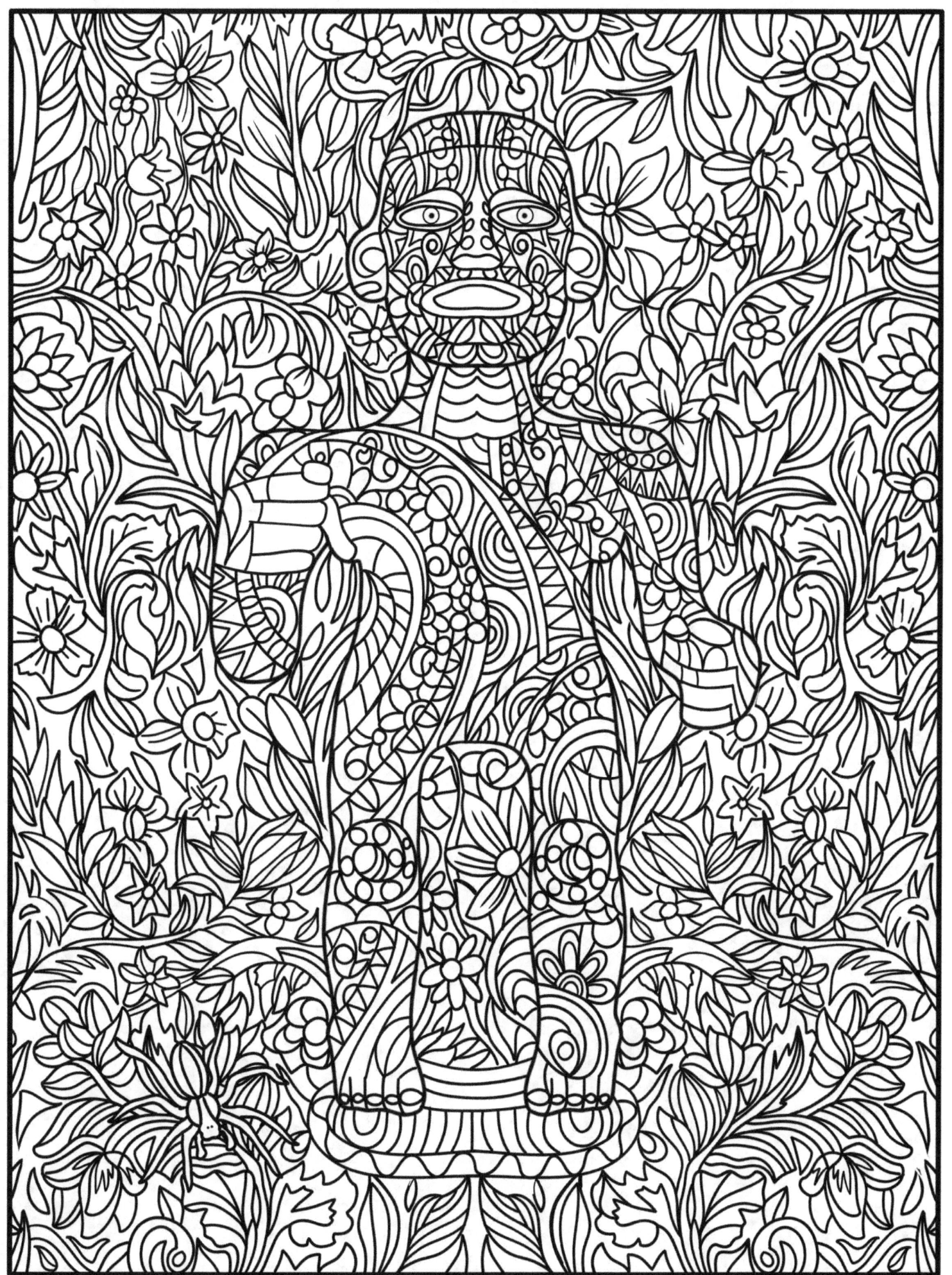

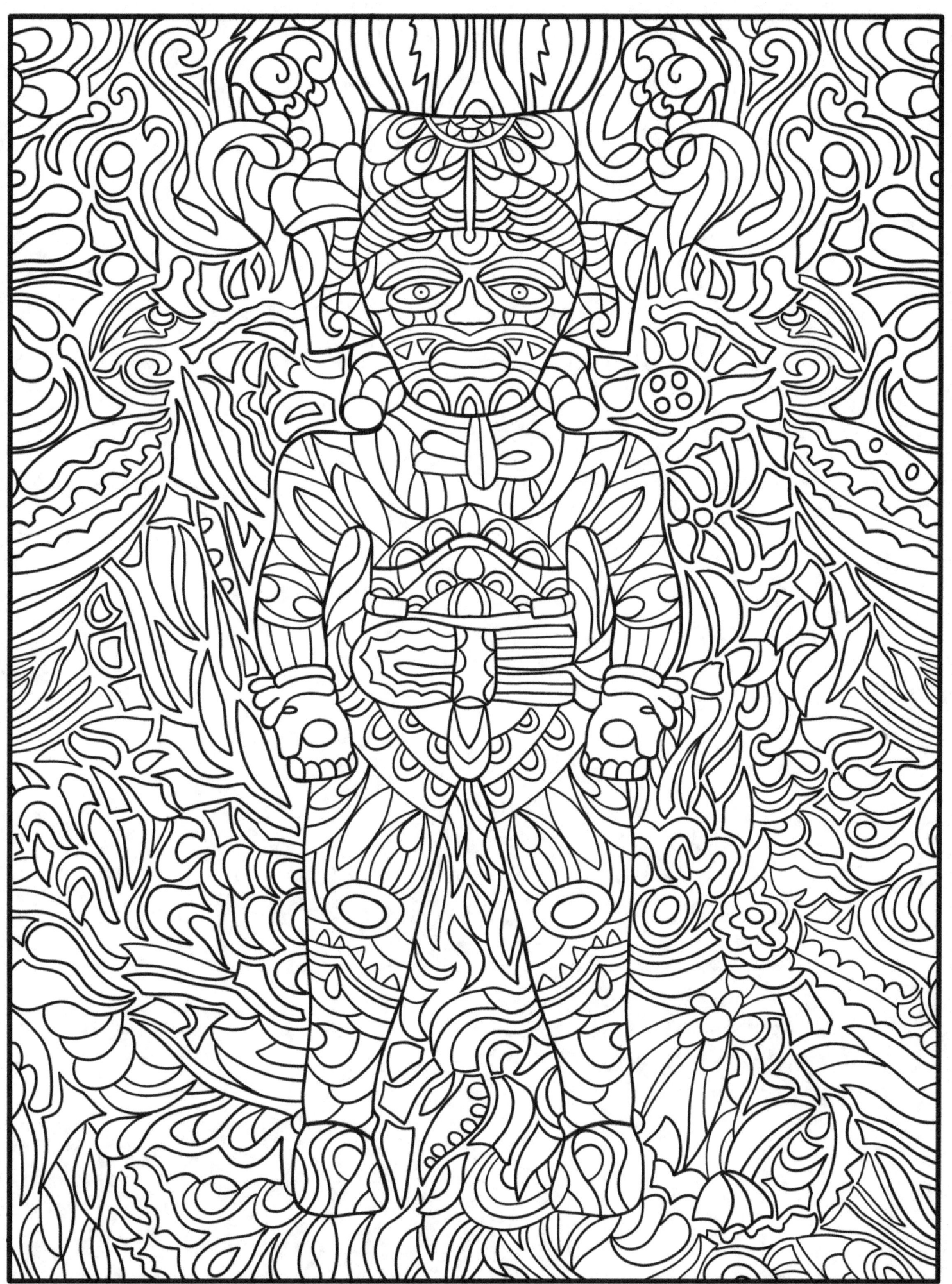

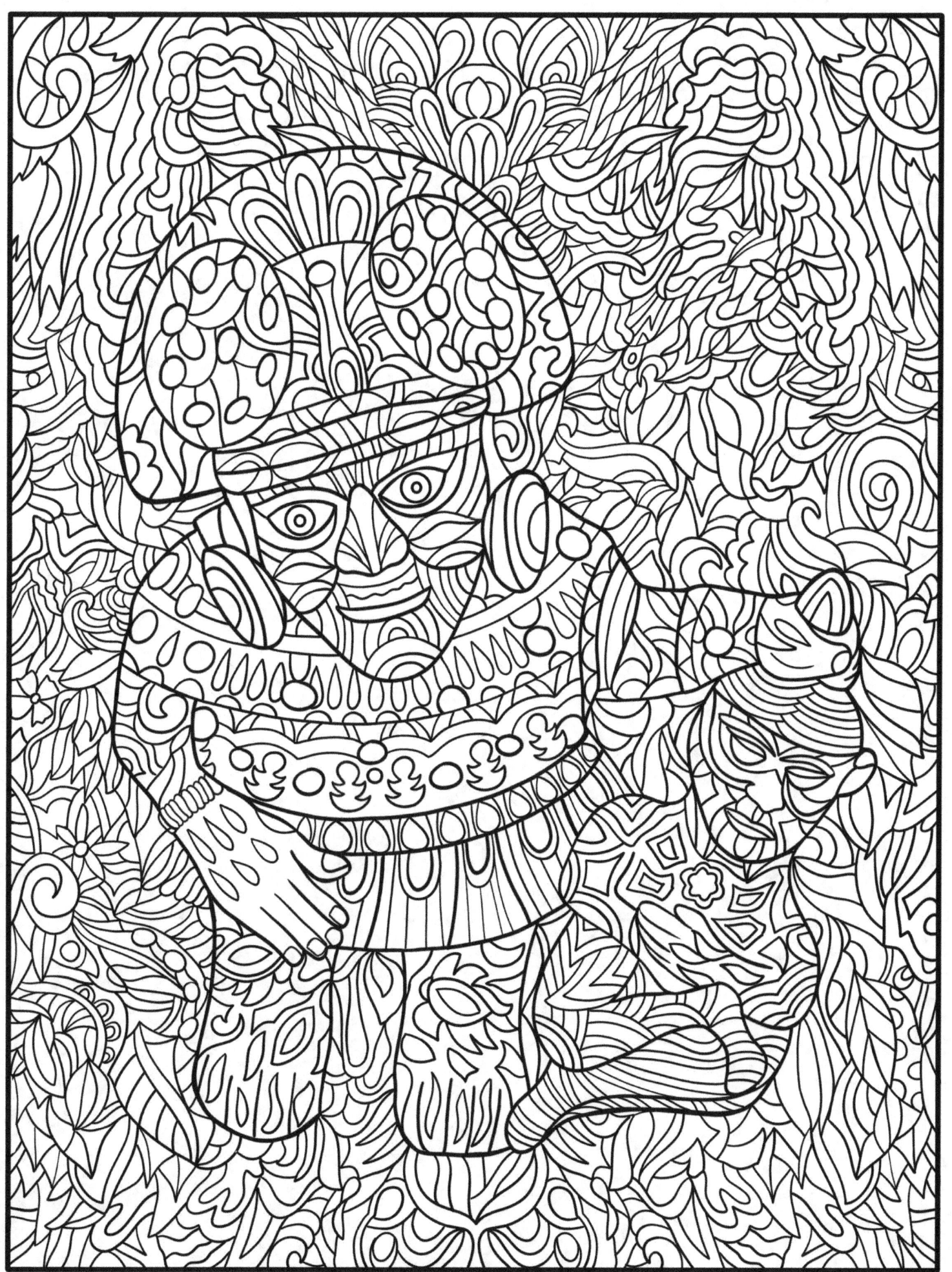

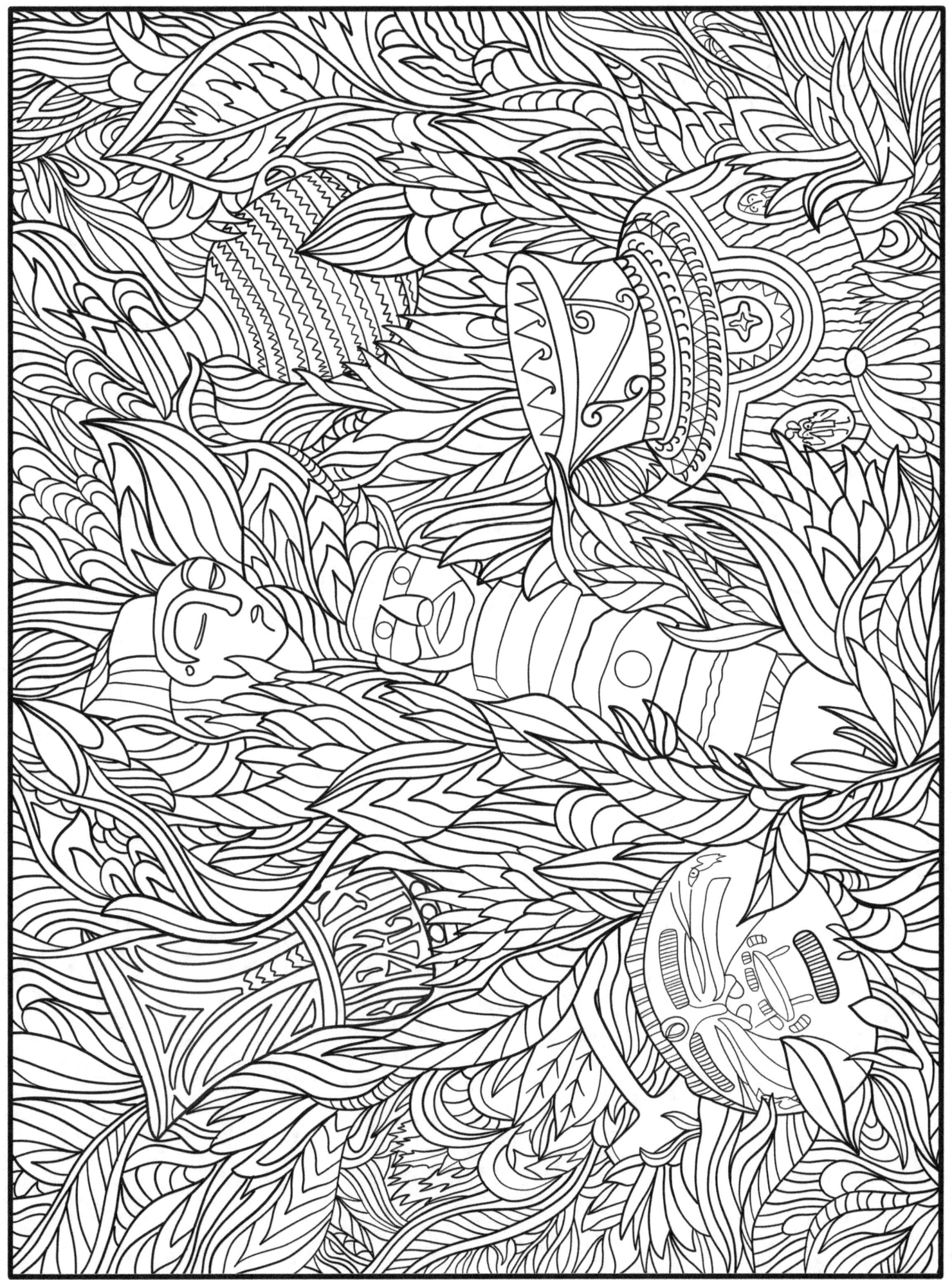

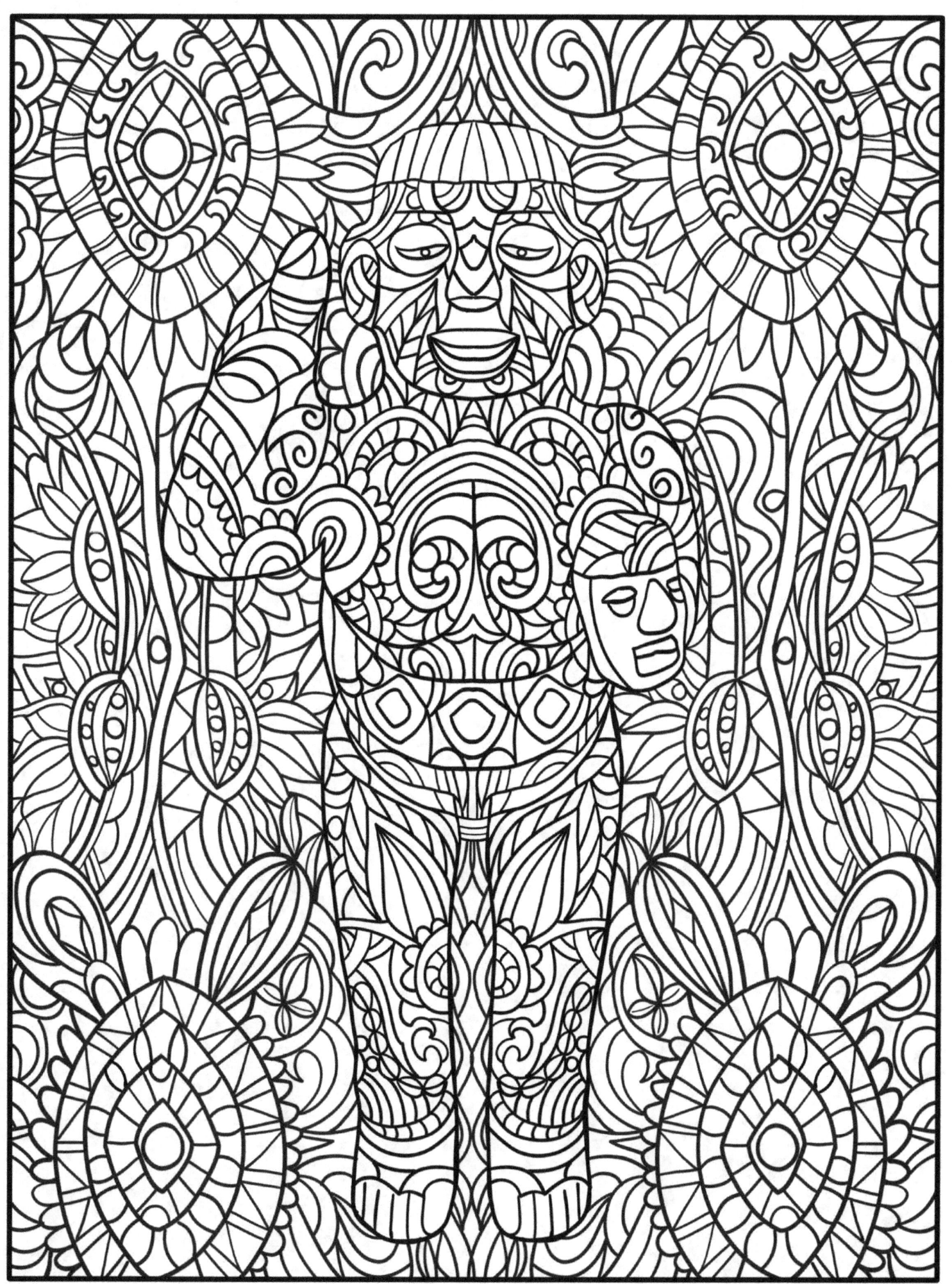

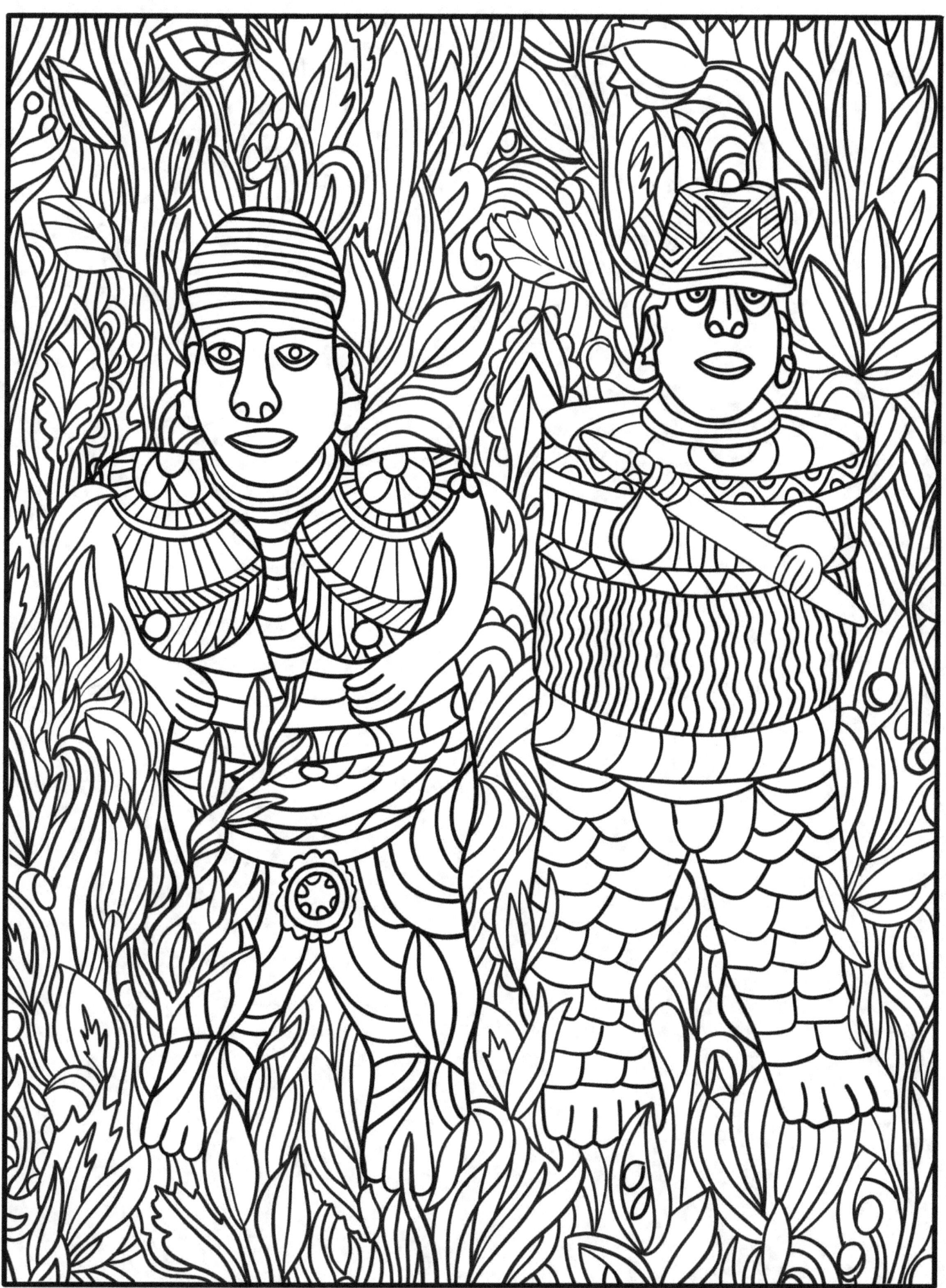

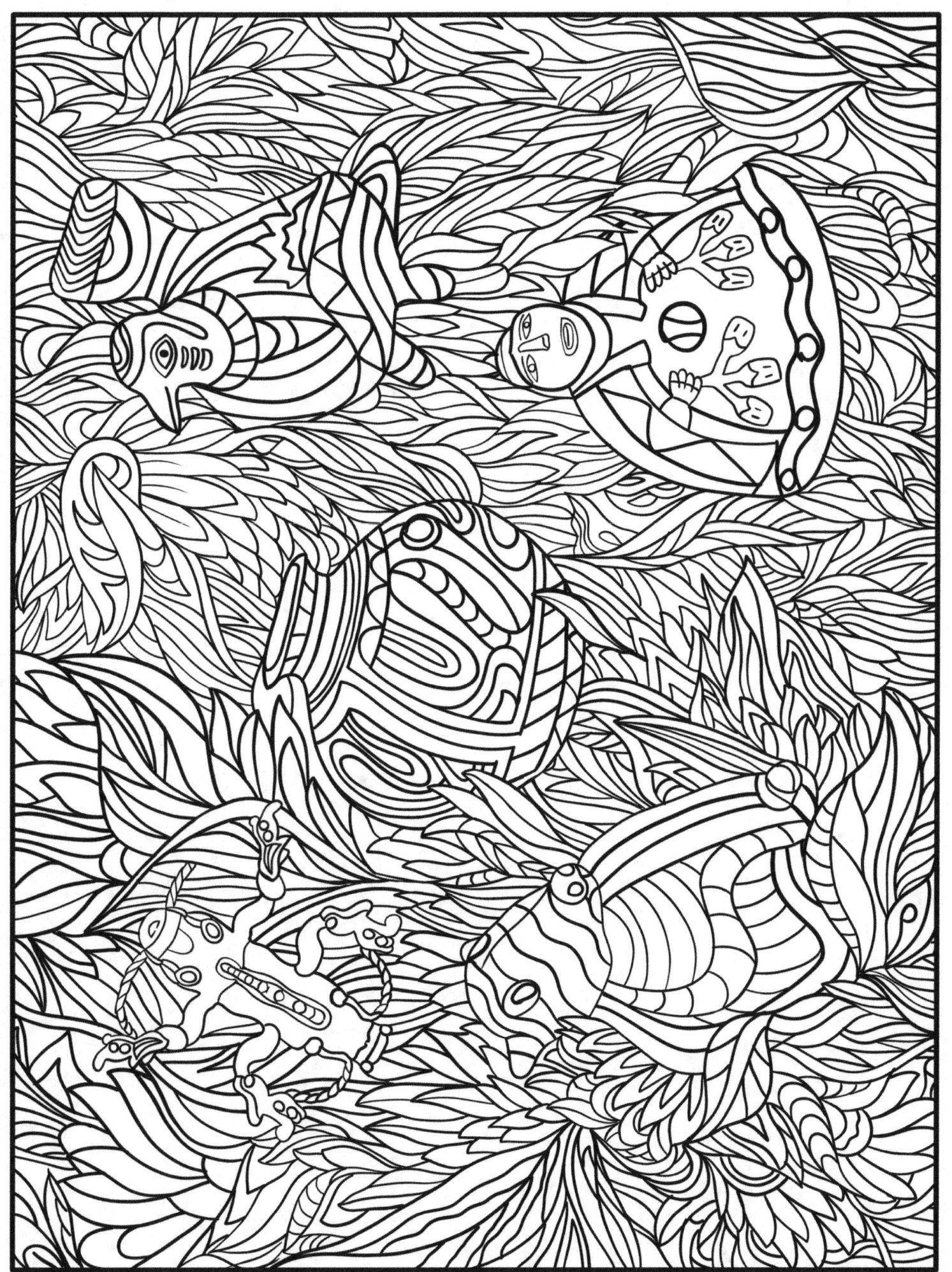

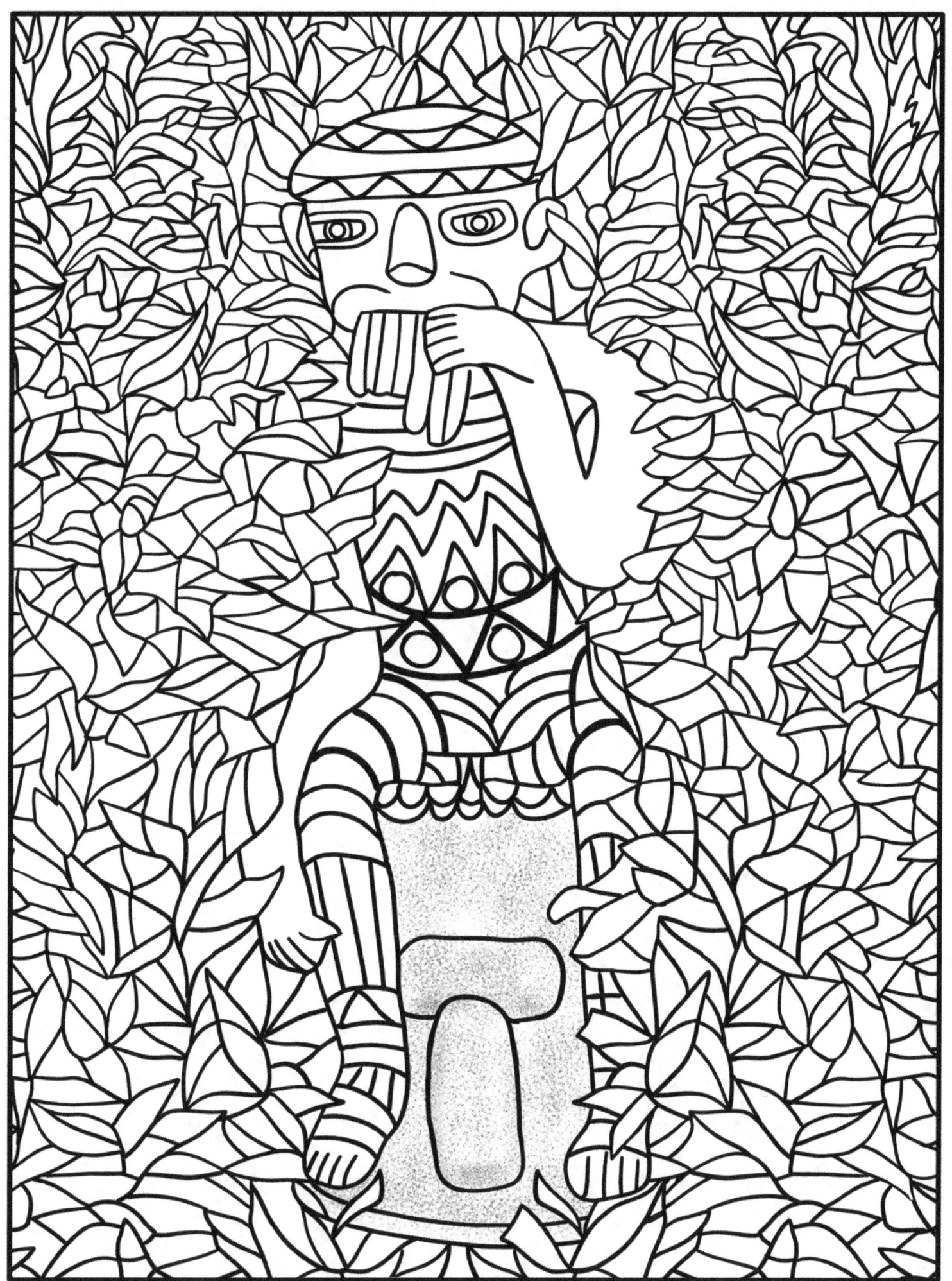

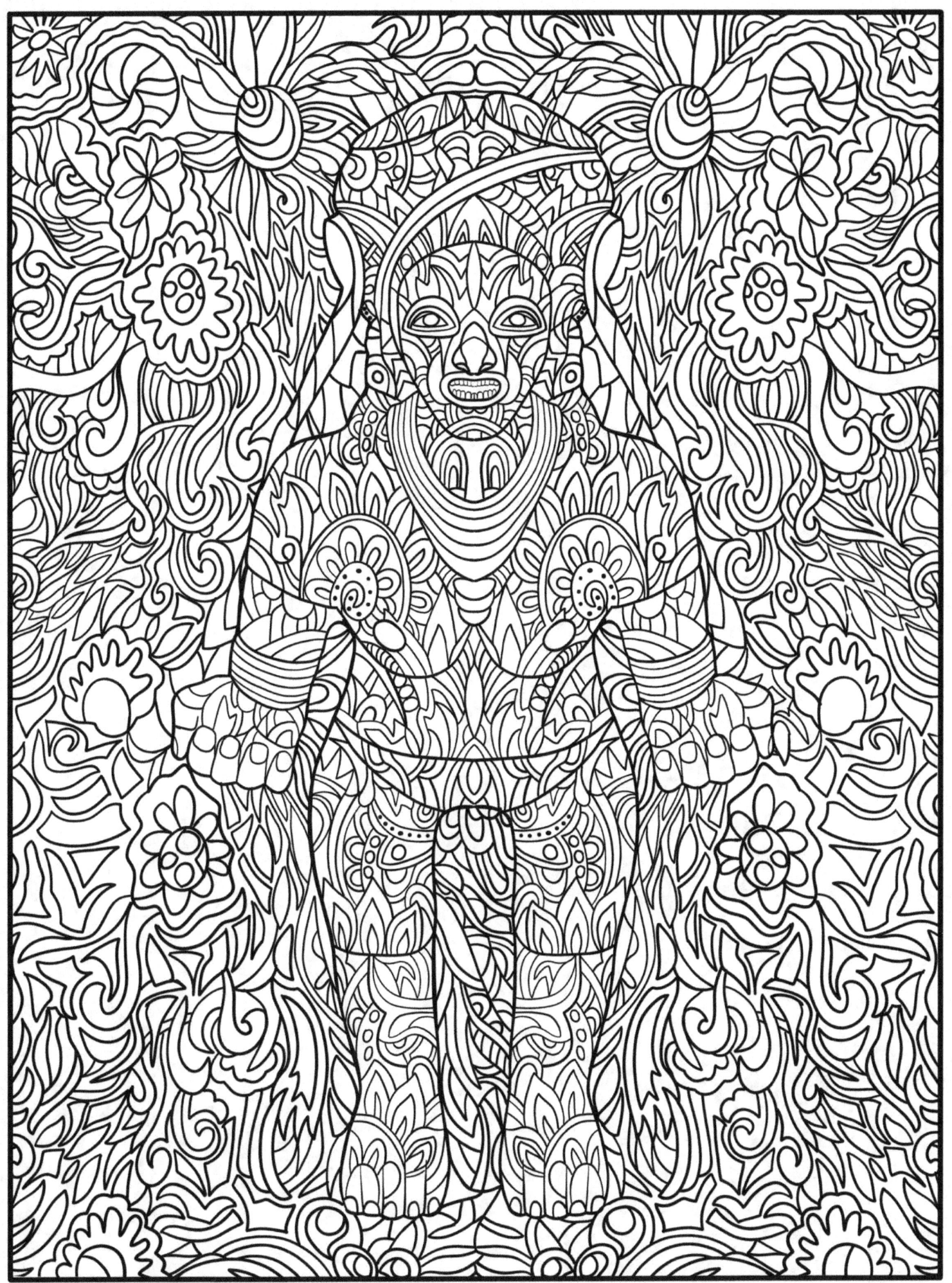

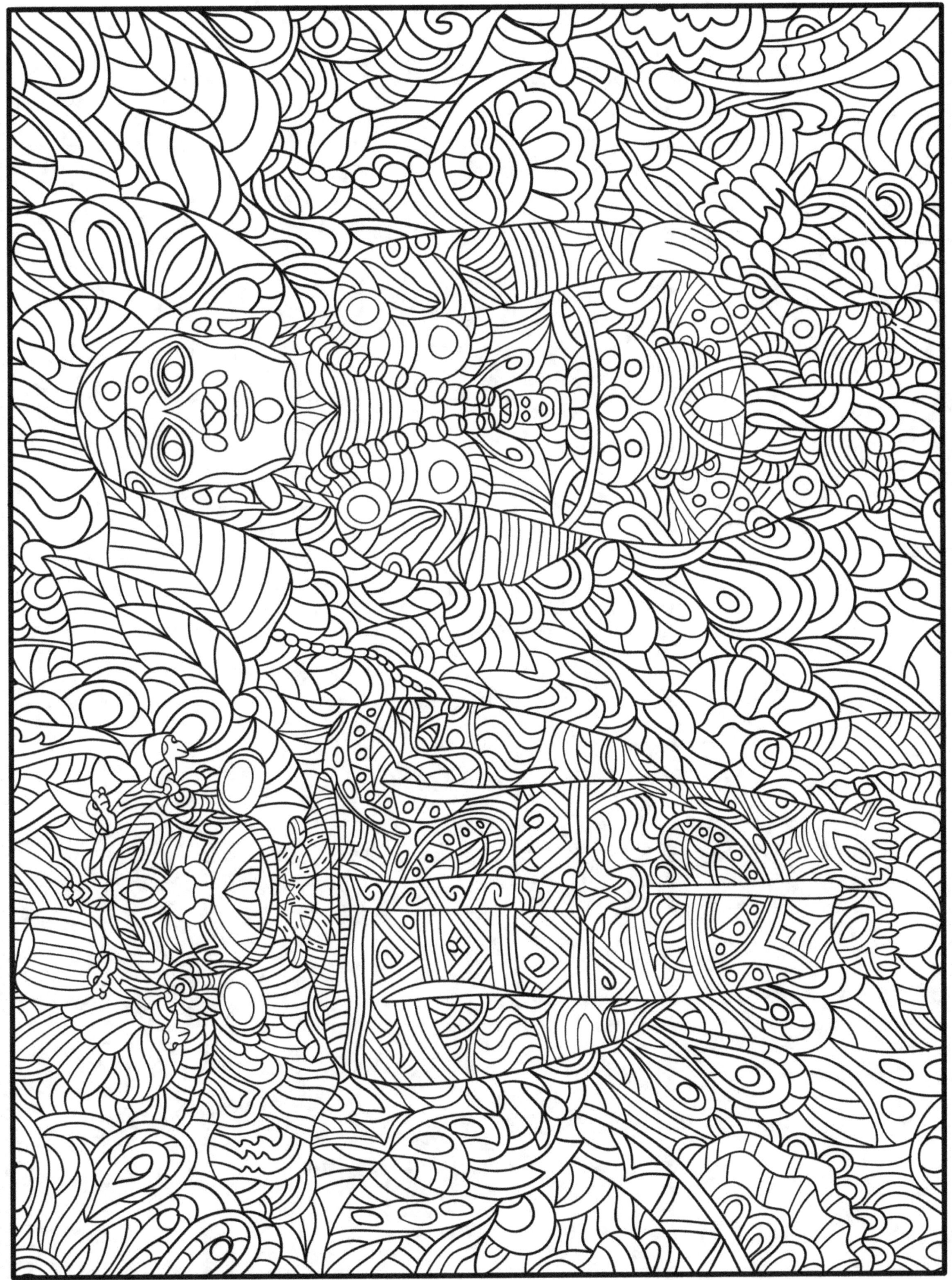

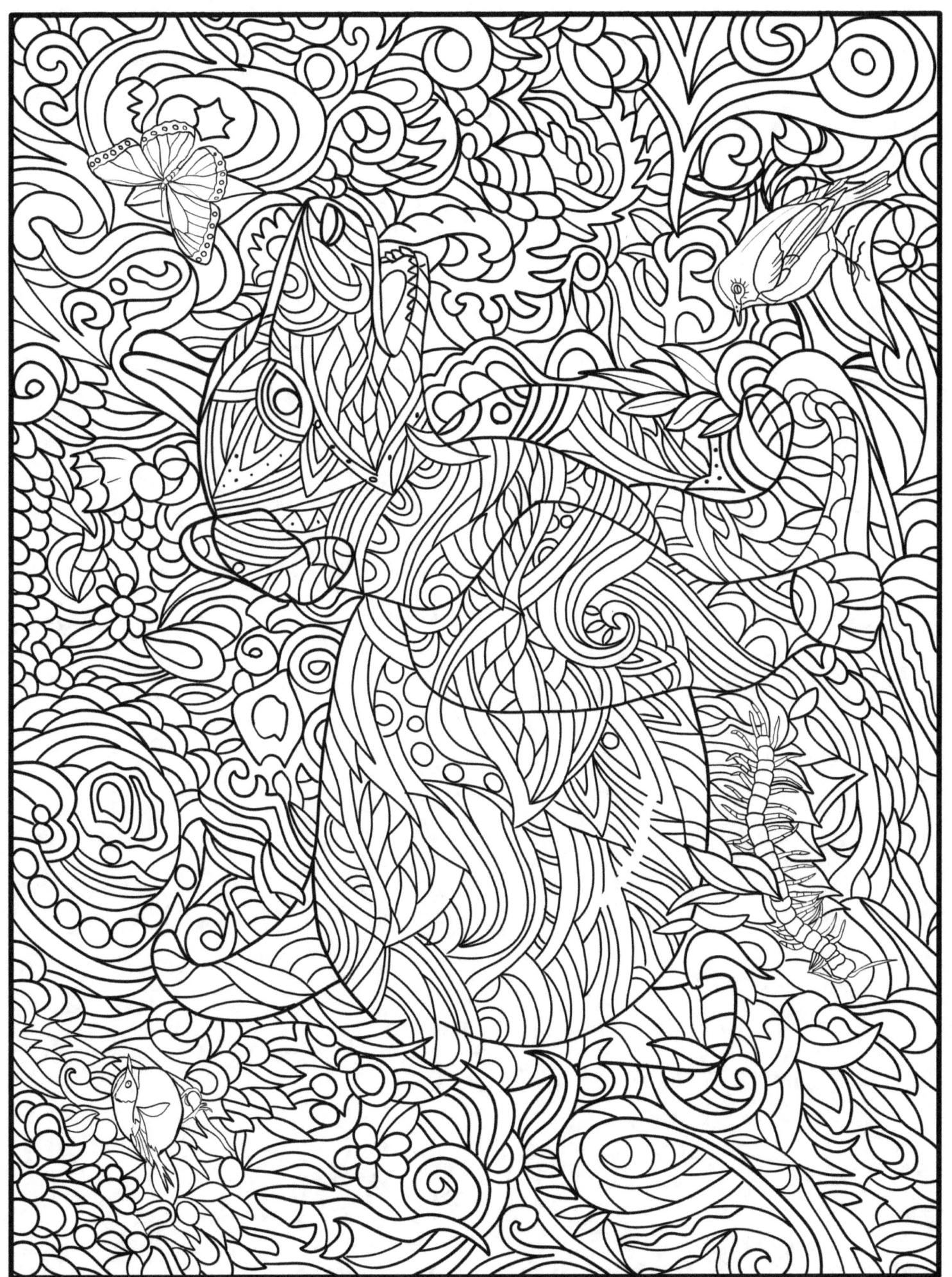

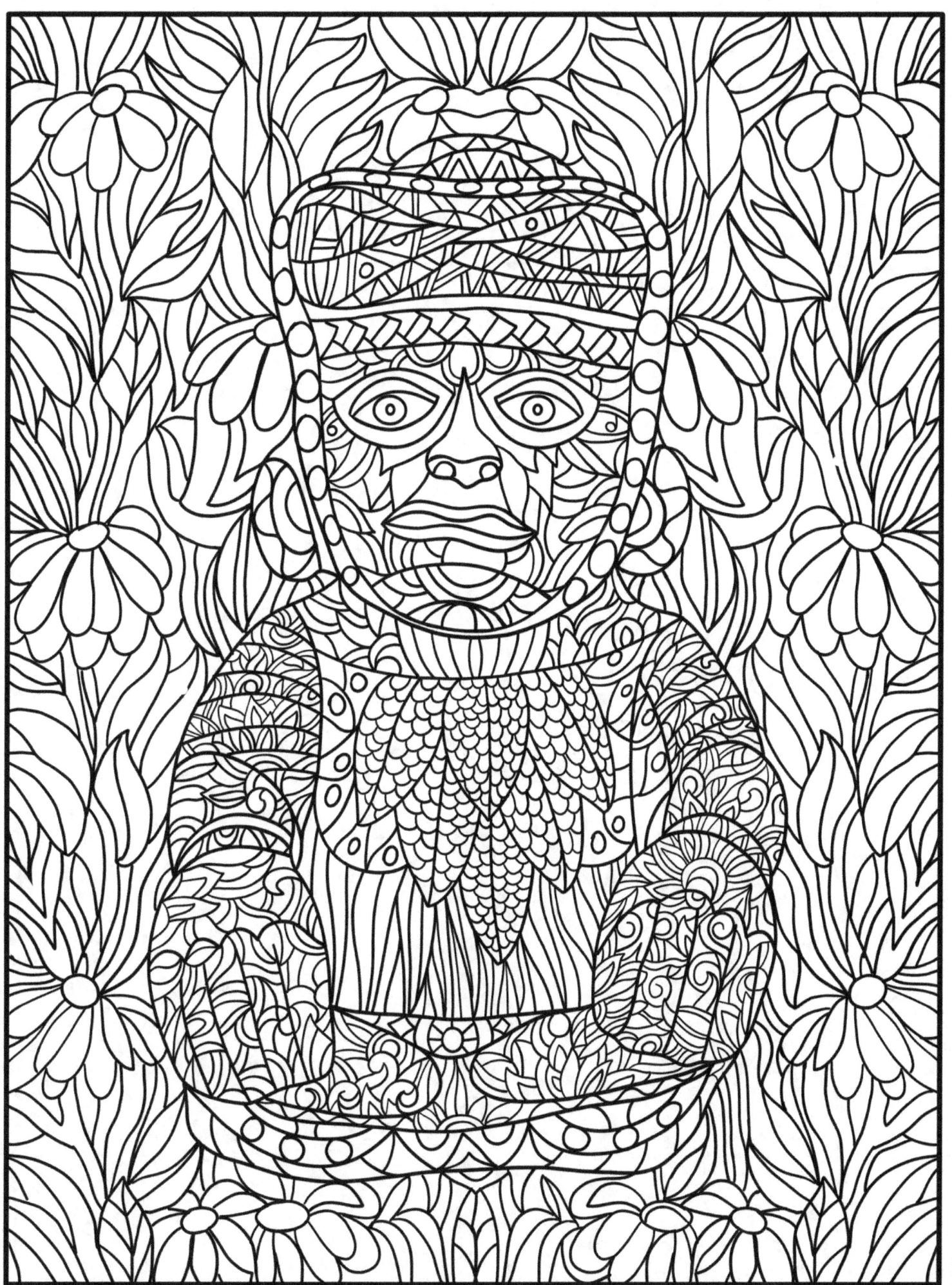

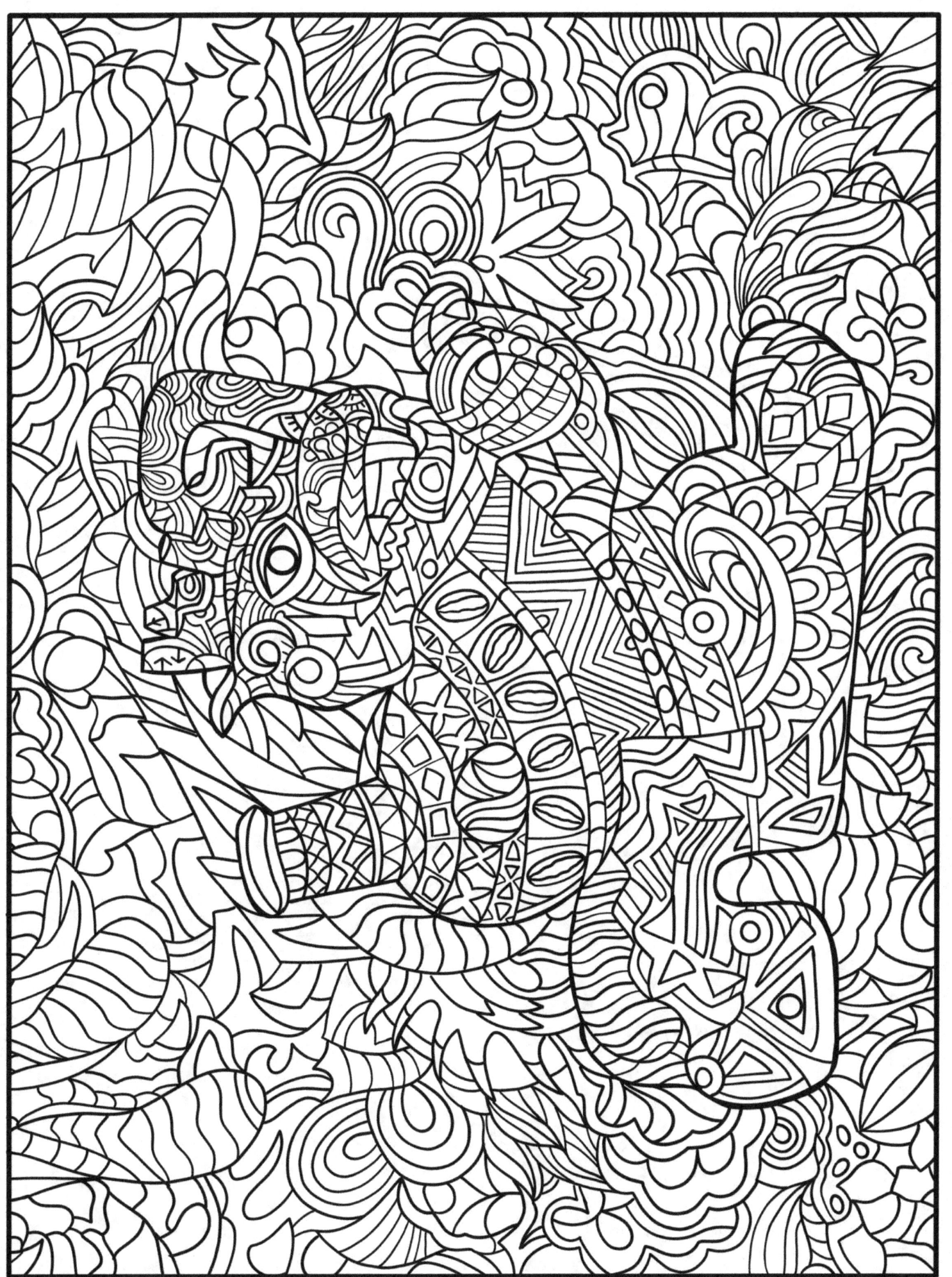

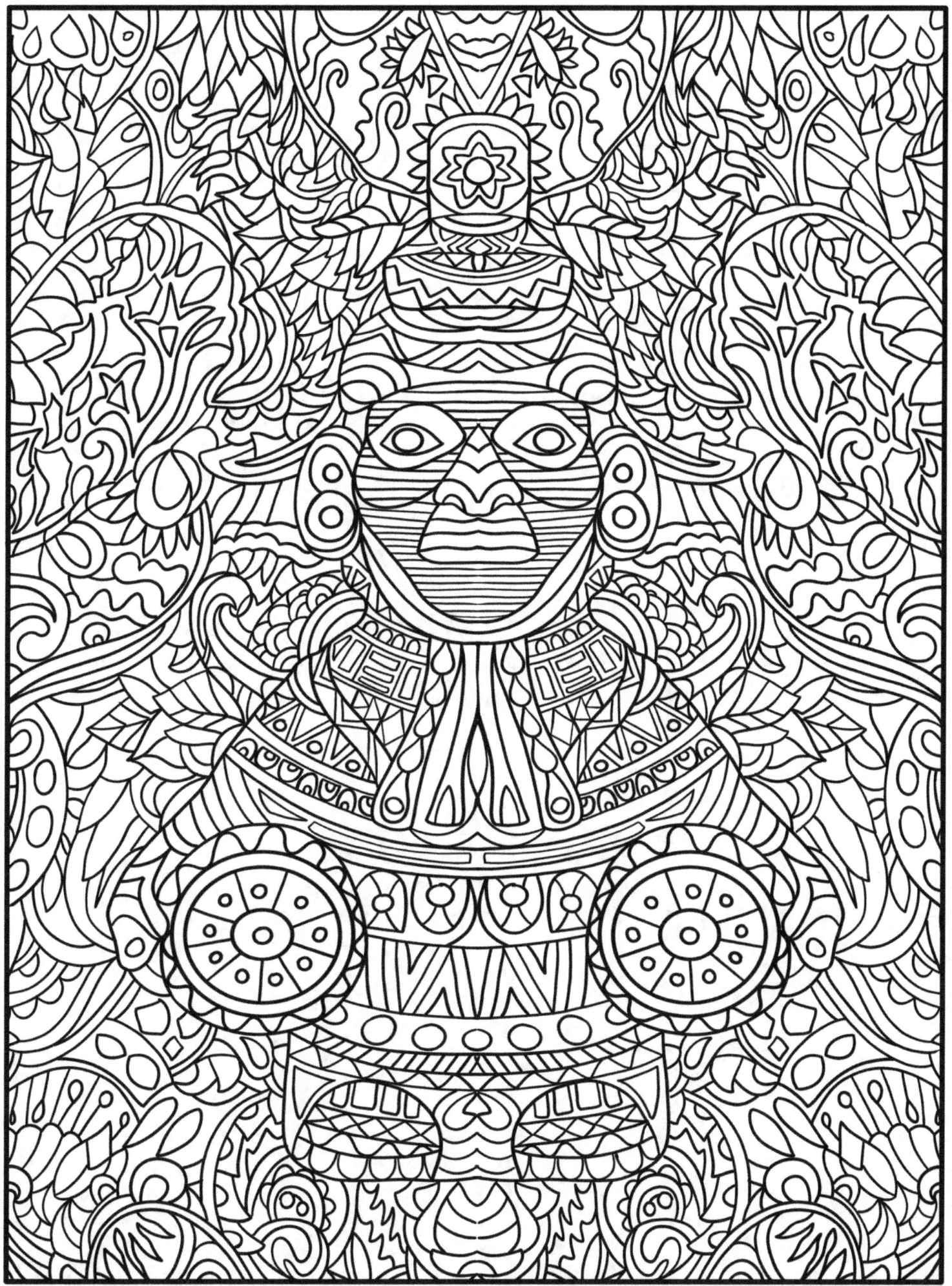

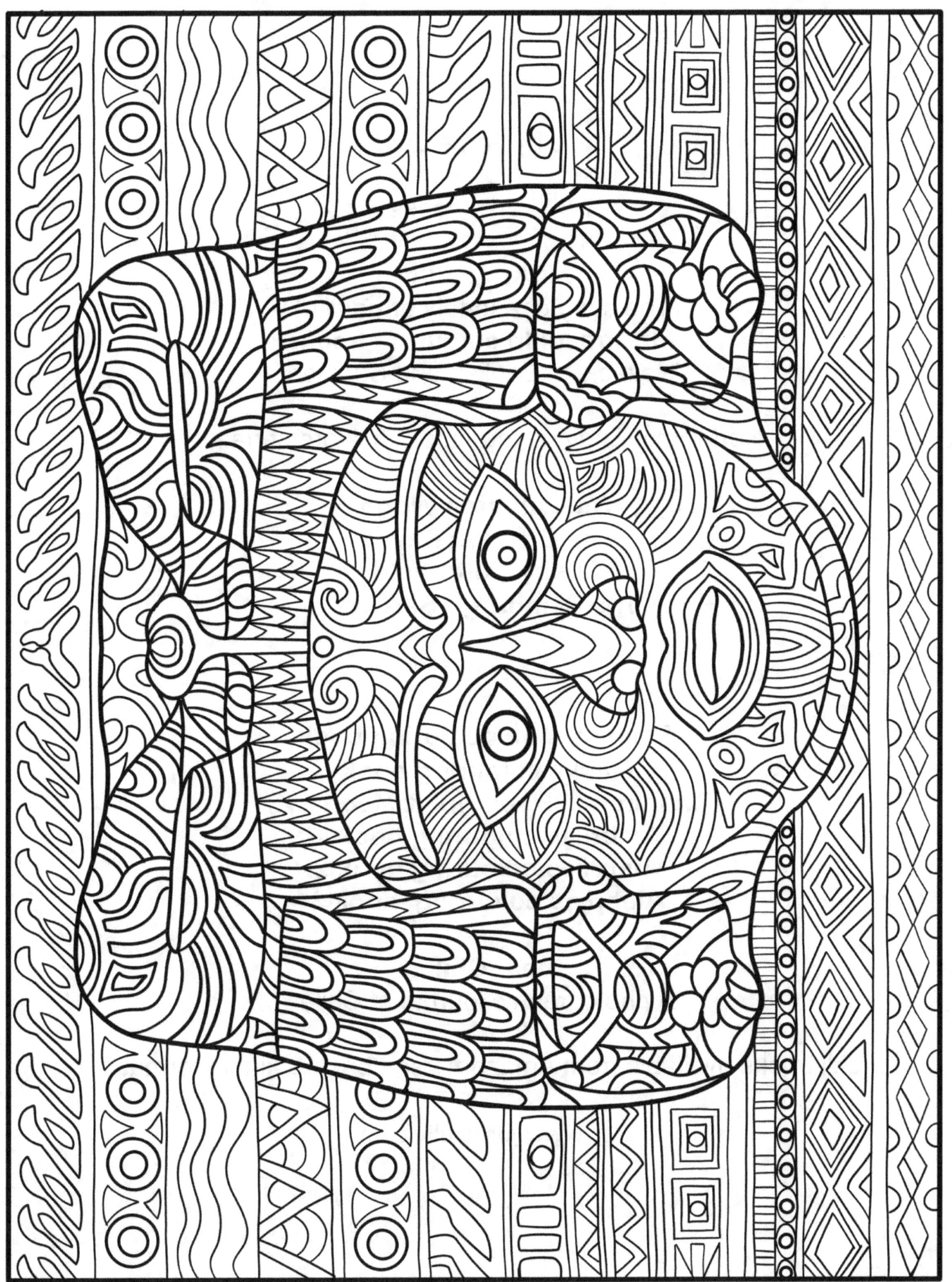

Also by Jorge Lulić

Children's books:

Mr Armadillo
(The story of a lonely armadillo)
Mr Armadillo colouring book
Available in English and Spanish

North East England legends & folklore series:

The Lambton Worm
The Blaydon Races
Cushy Butterfield
The Bamburgh Serpent

Other titles:

America Viva colouring book
Masks colouring book
(Inspired in Rapa Nui & Maori Art)
Alebrijes colouring book 1
Alebrijes colouring book 2
Alebrijes colouring book 3

Dear Chile
A photographic journal of Chile

All books available from Amazon – soft back & kindle format

www.jorgelulic.com